3-D MAGIC!

Simple Blocks, Striking Quilts

MARCI BAKER and SARA NEPHEW

C&T PUBLISHING
Another Maker Inspired!

Publisher: Amy Barrett-Daffin

Creative Director: Gailen Runge

Senior Editor: Roxane Cerda

Editor: Gailen Runge

Technical Editor: Helen Frost

Cover/Book Designer: April Mostek

Production Coordinator:Tim Manibusan

Illustrator: Mary Flynn

Photography Coordinator: Rachel Ackley

Photography by C&T Publishing, Inc.

Published by C&T Publishing, Inc., P.O. Box 1456, Lafayette, CA 94549

Library of Congress Cataloging-in-Publication Data

Names: Baker, Marcia L., author. | Nephew, Sara, author.

Title: 3-D magic! simple blocks, striking quilts / Marci Baker and Sara Nephew.

Description: Lafayette, CA : C&T Publishing, Another Maker Inspired, [2024]

| Summary: "Marci Baker and Sara Nephew teach quilters about the amazing

ability of using flat fabric and transforming it into cubes, holes, and

a 3-D landscape of the imagination. Included inside are seven quilt

projects and 13 3-D blocks with instructions that allow readers to

create the blocks in alternate sizes"-- Provided by publisher.

Identifiers: LCCN 2023030671 | ISBN 9781617459412 (trade paperback) | ISBN

9781617459429 (ebook)

Subjects: LCSH: Quilting--Patterns. | Quilting--Technique.

Classification: LCC TT835 .B2578 2024 | DDC 746.46/041--dc23/eng/20230724

LC record available at https://lccn.loc.gov/2023030671

Printed in China

10 9 8 7 6 5 4 3 2 1

DEDICATION

To quilters everywhere, my husband says
now I have friends all across the United States.
~ Sara ~

To my seven siblings, Team Mom and Dad.
We loved and learned through it all.
~ Marci ~

ACKNOWLEDGEMENTS

With special thanks to all the generous quilters who helped piece samples for this book and test the patterns: Laurie Biundo, Janet Blazekovich, Kristi Droese, Martha Ethridge, Kate McIntyre, Elaine Muzichuk, Alicia Sanchez, Pam Seaberg, Kathleen Springer, and Kathy Syring. Your talent shows!

When you try a different piecing method, when you do a pattern twice in order to experiment with a different colorway, when you slap the ruler down and cut around it differently, you are joining the ranks of creative, pioneering quilters everywhere, and contributing in a very large way to the quality and enjoyment presented by this book. It would be very difficult—no, impossible—to do this without you!

From Marci, thank you to everyone involved in this endeavor, for your patience and understanding on my schedule or lack thereof for this project. You followed along while I was in the season of taking care of elderly parents. For that I am so grateful. Because of your talents, I know this book has been worth the wait!

Let the magic begin...

CONTENTS

Preface
A Different Angle

This book is about the amazing ability of flat fabric to look like actual cubes, holes, even a three-dimensional landscape of the imagination. You can do it without crumpling, folding, or bunching material, but just by choosing light, medium, and dark fabrics.

Drafting a view of a proposed project, architects can use 60° angles to create, on paper, buildings with a look of depth, and the building contractor can use the drawings as a preliminary idea of the work. Machinists can use the 60° drawings as a helpful projection of what a part they are making on their computer-controlled machine will look like. All this comes from using different angles to suggest shape and dimension.

Most quilters are comfortable cutting squares, rectangles, and triangles (90° and 45° angles), but patterns using 60°, 30°, and 120° angles are less common. Baby Blocks or Tumbling Blocks, Grandmother's Flower Garden, plus 6-pointed stars are traditional and the most familiar 60° patterns.

 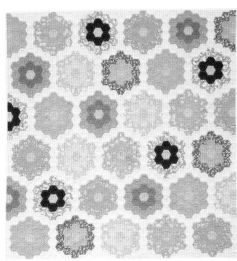 

Now we have new tools that help us to explore more possibilities for quilts using these angles. We can be artists using simple blocks or take our work to a new level using a wide variety! If you are interested in a couple of artist's experiments with 60° illusions and visual dimension, see work by M. C. Escher and some pieces by Victor Vasarely.

This book takes a small number of geometric shapes that are easy to make and shows how to use them to create 3-D illusions as quilts. Quick methods are given so many quilts can be produced easily. Other examples show quilts made like paintings, with colors and shapes inserted and combined after some contemplation. We hope you enjoy looking at the possibilities so that you'll be inspired to try your own ideas.

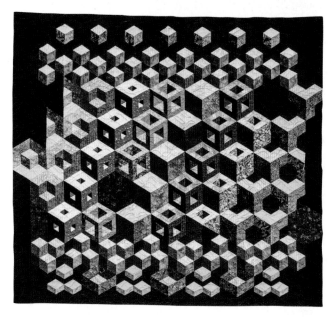

INTRODUCTION
Using this Book

To create the quilts shown in this book, we present the basic design ideas and various methods used for these quilts. First, we discuss facts about fabrics to choose, because specific characteristics of fabric can really affect the success of your project. You may find that a quick trip to the quilt shop is in order to select the right material. Or it may require a more extensive shop hop. Oh well, someone has to do it.

Next, we give directions for 13 block designs, offered in three sizes each. They finish at 9″, 7″, and 5″ across. Just as in traditional square blocks, these hexagonal designs will fit together into a quilt. They can be all the same block or a variety of blocks.

Try a few blocks to get a feel for the different piecing techniques. Rotary cutting the individual shapes is the basic technique. This is Sara's favorite method because she can enjoy making blocks one at a time, using scraps of fabric, often made with scraps of her time. We provide an alternate speed-piecing method for blocks that have several units with the same fabric. Marci enjoys this technique because she dives in and creates a lot of units all at once.

To make the projects, you position the blocks desired and fill the edges of the quilt with half-block shapes and triangle halves. The piecing methods avoid Y-seams or set-in seams. The simplicity of the piecing compared to the dramatic 3-D effect is where the magic happens.

We include seven different quilt projects with complete step-by-step directions. Jump right in and start making one of these quilts. Or consider using one or more blocks for a design of your own.

The book also includes a gallery of quilts, a wide variety of creations made by us and other quilters. These quilters have so generously tested our instructions, provided feedback when needed, and shared their projects with all of us. Their ideas may give you a great new inspiration. That's exciting! Or even just looking at the beauties in the gallery may add a few minutes of pleasure to soothe your day.

The last bits of information in the book are dry but necessary: the cutting instructions for the shapes, full-size templates, and for designing your own quilt, a cut-and-paste grid with block drawings.

With all that we have included for your success, we hope you enjoy this book and creating your own 3-D magic.

Tools

The tools needed to rotary cut the shapes in this book are very basic. We list our favorite brands in parentheses following each item.

- **Rotary cutter** (OLFA) — The 45mm size is the best for speed and safety.

- **Self-healing mat** (OLFA) — Marci uses the blank side of the mat to eliminate conflict between 90° and 60° lines.

- **6″ × 12″ or 6″ × 24″ ruler** (Omnigrid or Creative Grids) for cutting straight strips for strip piecing.

- **60° ruler** (Clearview Triangle 60° ruler or Clearview Triangle Super 60° ruler by C&T Publishing) for cutting the shapes (optional)

- **Corner-trimming tool** (Corner Cut 60 2-in-1 Sewing Tool by C&T Publishing) for trimming shapes (optional)

NOTE We recommend using the Clearview Triangle rulers. We know there are other 60° rulers available, but other rulers, especially those with a blunt tip, measure differently than what is shown here. If you choose to use another manufacturer's ruler, be sure to check your work as you go. The Clearview Triangle rulers are available from C&T Publishing (ctpub.com). If you don't want to work with a triangle ruler, we provide templates at the back of the book to use to cut the shapes.

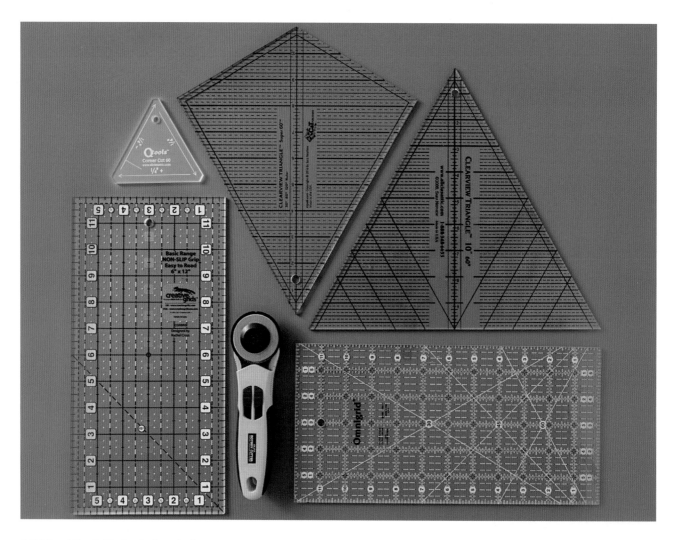

Fabric Choices

WHAT MATERIAL WORKS BEST?

Of course, the preferred fabric for quilts is light- to medium-weight cotton. Use the best quality you can afford. Besides regular cottons found in quilt shops, Sara has experimented with lighter-weight cotton upholstery fabrics.

Perhaps you already have a large collection of yardage and scraps. Your local quilt shop also has plenty. Or if you have time and the inclination, you can haunt thrift shops and garage sales like Sara does, for "new" fabrics. It's best to avoid used clothing for two reasons: first, it's a lot of trouble to take garments apart for what may be small pieces; and second, the fabric may be too old to wear well in a quilt. This could result in holes in a quilt that are unfortunately *not* an illusion.

Once you have your fabric selected, the next question is to wash or not wash. Sara prewashes her fabric, while Marci does not. See our reasons for why we choose what we do listed below. You may find that you want to change your routine to fit your needs (not your first quilt teacher's or your quilting friends' needs.)

WHAT IS VALUE?

Wherever you are buying your fabric, the main aspect to selecting fabric for 3-D illusion quilts is the contrast in value, light, medium, or dark, not the color. The more dramatic the contrast between fabric values, the more realistic the 3-D illusion.

From experience we find that most quilters fit into one of two categories. Either they own mostly light-valued fabric and dark-valued fabric, which is great for many traditional quilt patterns because the high contrast makes the design stand out. We call them Traditional quilters.

Other quilters own all medium colors because they love color and enjoy handling and working with bright, intense colors. These we call Jewel-Tone quilters.

For successful 3-D illusions, you need both groupings. That is, your fabric collection needs to include light and dark and medium. Actually, to artistically improve a quilt, whether for a 3-D illusion or not, including a variety of light, medium, and dark valued fabrics throughout creates movement and interest across the design. So, you now have permission and validation to expand your fabrics so you have all that you need, both the Traditional collection and the Jewel-Tone collection.

TO WASH OR NOT TO WASH

Sara washes because she likes the light finish. (She lightly washes the fabric when she brings it home, before filing it into her stash.)

Marci does not wash ahead. She wants to dive right in.

REASONS TO WASH

• Shrinks the fabric

• Removes some of the finish

• Releases excess dyes to prevent running

• Reduces chemicals

REASONS NOT TO WASH

• Saves time

• Finish helps fabric feed through the sewing machine easily

• Quilt can be washed later using Color Catchers by Shout

Whether washing before or after, use Color Catchers by Shout to determine if the dye is still running. If so, it may require another wash.

A fabric is not light, medium, or dark on its own, rather only when it is compared to another fabric. It is all relative. When fabrics are displayed next to each other, then they can be compared and viewed using different tools and methods.

There are some items that are somewhat helpful in judging value. Pieces of colored plastic that you look through to help you see value versus color are available; red works best on cool tones (green, blue, violet) and green works best on warm tones (red, orange, and yellow). Try using the peep-hole for a door, or binoculars—looked through backwards—and other various methods to help see fabric from a distance, which can make differences in value stand out. We have found that the best tools for us are our eyes. To see the lightness or darkness of fabric, you just need to narrow your eyes. This means squeeze your eyes almost shut until you can barely see. That means squint! The view darkens, and areas of dark and light simplify.

To easily find light, medium, and dark for your 3-D illusions, follow this simple procedure that relies on squinting:

1 First choose a fabric that is either very light or very dark. Then choose the opposite. You may wish to squint a bit as you are doing this. Place the two fabrics next to or slightly over each other.

2 Spread out the fabrics as necessary so they are not bulky, as this might cause one fabric to cast a shadow over the other. Next try to choose a fabric that is exactly in between your light and your dark. Place this fabric across your light and dark, as a horizontal bar across two vertical bars.

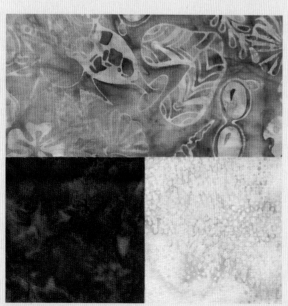

3 Squint and notice the contrast with the light and with the dark. Now put it vertically between the light and dark fabrics. Then squint at your fabrics. Is the medium closer in value to the dark or to the light? Exactly halfway would be ideal.

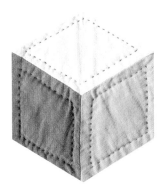

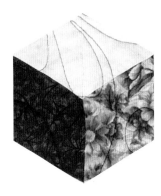

Think of this as if it were stairs. If you were walking up some stairs, you want the stairs to be exactly the same height, not one stair huge and one stair only as thick as a little edge to trip over. If your medium is very close to the light or the dark in your block, it creates the look of wings instead of looking like a cube.

When the values are evenly spaced like the stair steps, the 3-D design is distinct.

When your light is really light and your dark is really dark, and your medium is exactly in between, you will achieve a strong 3-D illusion of cubes.

The available fabrics do not always create a strong design. Don't stress over finding that perfect fabric, rather know that the strong illusions will help carry the weaker combinations. Another thing to realize when struggling on a selection, the groupings that are not as strong also add interest to the quilt.

This is Marci's first Tumbling Blocks quilt. She thought she was doing a color study, only to find that it was really a value study. These were the fabrics available to her at local quilt shops in 1987. A couple of the groupings work well, and those that don't are okay, too. There is interest across the design because of the "missed" value choices. See the diagonal fuchsia line, and the dark zigzag in the green, blue, and purple? Yet you probably saw tumbling blocks before those elements.

You can make a quilt from just three fabrics, with a strong illusion throughout. Or you can work with various light-medium-dark combinations for a play of color, texture, and details across the quilt. To quickly choose values for 3-D illusions with confidence, use Marci's method of squinting and a grayscale, page 16. And to discover even more about value and how to place a large group of fabrics in value order, use Sara's value chart exercise, page 14.

These three prints are examples of the range in sizes.

WHAT SIZE OF PRINT?

When you begin selecting fabric for a 3-D illusion, know that the size of the print, especially high-contrast designs, affects the perceived value.

First, eliminate high-contrast, large prints. These fabrics are great for some other uses, but they do not contribute to a look of dimension. Instead, they break up the look of the shapes.

Medium-size prints can sometimes be high contrast with light and dark in a pattern. Since your eye tends to mix and blend the elements, we recommend they be used with discretion and sparingly. When used effectively, these patterns can add a lot of charm to the illusion.

Small prints work well because they appear as a consistent, overall value. Having similar prints throughout helps tie the quilt together. For example, if you choose to use one plaid, it would look even better to have three or more to blend the plaids across the quilt. The same can be said for any motif, like stripes, small botanicals, or dots, that stands out in the crowd of the selected fabrics.

Solids are excellent, and batiks are great, sometimes adding the look of rock or concrete to an illusory structure. Because these fabrics in general are a consistent value, they provide a definite line to contrast with the other fabrics. The more solid-looking the fabrics are, the stronger the 3-D effect can be, if the values are chosen well.

A BIGGER CHALLENGE—ADDING BACKGROUND

You may want to go beyond a 3-D shape in light, medium, and dark (designs like Honeycomb Waffle, page 22, and Hollow Cube, page 35, which fit together edge to edge) and put your shape into empty space, floating on a background.

Some designs have an element of space. Look at Sugar Cube (page 60), Arches and Asteroids (page 64), and Netcube (page 67). There is now a need for four values: light, medium, dark, and background. You can make the background darker than the cube, lighter than the cube, or a texture or color that will stand out from your 3-D figure. *Honey* Quilt, shown here, is an excellent example of contrast in texture. The high-contrast print fabric allows the blocks to stand out, even though a couple of the fabrics are close in value.

Another option available to you is the direction of the light source. Three-dimensional designs are created by giving the illusion of light coming from a specific direction. The blocks and most of the quilts in this book have a light source shining from the upper left. This means the light fabric is on top, the dark is on the right, and the medium is on the left. However, the direction can be changed. Kate McIntyre decided to have the light shine from the right so the dark is on the left, in her quilt Jamboree, page 72. We made a choice of light source. And you can choose, too.

You may find you were following our instructions but accidently made blocks with the value reversed. It is just fine as long as you are consistent throughout the project. Otherwise, the viewer may be perplexed with 3-D confusion rather than amazed at your 3-D illusion.

To evaluate your work as you go, step back and look at the overall effect, squint at the blocks on the wall, or have a friend look at them. Most likely discrepancies will appear. Sara found one in Marci's projects when she shared a photograph of the work in progress. Luckily it was before all of the blocks were sewn together. The more you work with these illusions, the better you will get at it. Just page through the Gallery, beginning on page 64, to see the different effects we all have created. This work is fun, striking, and impressive!

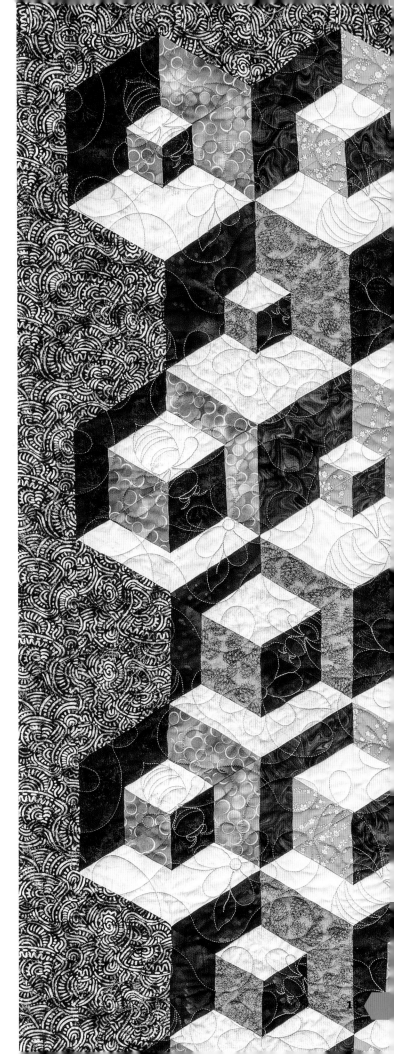

Honey Quilt detail

Practice Seeing Value

Sara's Value Chart

If you want to develop your ability to choose fabrics that give an illusion of 3-D, it can be fun and instructive to create a value chart. You may even want to do this out of fabrics you are auditioning for a quilt. This gives you more control over the project and makes choosing a variety of good value combinations easier.

The goal is to start with a group of fabrics and sort them light to dark. Once they are placed in order, groupings of light, medium, and dark can be selected easily.

Here is how to make a value chart:

First, gather 12–15 different fabrics you might use. Make sure you have a range of light, medium, and dark fabrics with no high-contrast large prints. The exercise can be done with whole pieces of fabric or with small strips of fabric to keep as a reference for the project. If using the strips, gather glue, tape or a stapler, and 2 pieces of cardstock or a piece of cardboard (8˝ × 20˝ or so) to make the fabric sample chart.

Second, prepare the fabrics for comparison. Fold each large piece so that it is flat enough to not cast a shadow when placed on top of another piece of fabric. Or, cut a small strip (1½˝ × 6˝ or so) from each fabric. This should be large enough so that fabric still shows when they are slightly overlapping. Make sure the edges are clean cut, not torn or frayed, as clean edges make comparisons easier.

Third, place the fabric pieces/strips overlapping each other to create a gradation of values. Start at the dark end by placing the very darkest fabric. Then select the next fabric, just lighter than the darkest one. Continue building through the mediums and up to the lightest fabric. Remember to slightly overlap the fabrics while arranging, as seeing some background in between fabrics is very confusing.

When placing a new fabric, use the technique shared on page 10 where the new fabric is placed across the other fabrics so it can be compared to all of them. Notice the paisley print placement.

Squint and see where the best fit would be. Slide the piece in place. Squint again.

You will notice when a particular strip jumps to your attention. It will look like a stripe with strong lines on both sides. This usually means it's in the wrong position and needs to be moved toward darker or lighter. Notice the orange strip and paisley strip in the first photo. By swapping those two fabrics, the order is smoother.

Why "usually"? Certain colors are warmer, and will look lighter because of this. When your eyes are wide open, red, yellow, orange, and even some purples, have a fire of their own inside. They will look right in one position. But when you squint at them, you can see how much darker they are and you may need to move their position. Even though colors like these can be a little confusing, they add a lot to every design.

When your value range is a smooth gradation from light to dark, record the results. If working with large fabric pieces, take a photo. If working with the fabric strips, adhere them to the cardstock or cardboard. Again, overlap them slightly so you don't see the background.

Now you can choose three fabrics for a 3-D effect. If you choose one from the dark end, one from the light end, and one from in between, you'll most likely have a strong 3-D effect. Or choose from the middle and light and one in between to make a lighter 3-D block, or from the dark and middle and one in between to make a dark 3-D block. It's fun to make a sun-splashed look with some dark blocks and some light blocks, all in 3-D. Here is how this grouping of fabrics worked for scrappy tumbling blocks.

Remember, that strong 3-D combinations will help carry the weaker 3-D selections. So don't stress. Have fun playing with the fabrics. View your choices from a distance. See if anything looks out of place in this photo. There are two blocks that have been rotated (light is not on top) and cause tension in the design. The more you work with value, the better you will get at producing a 3-D illusion. And the better all your quilts will look, as you become more confident with value.

Quick Value Choices Using Grayscale

One simple tool that Marci uses is a grayscale. Along the edge of this page, is a series of gray sections in order by value, light to dark. With this standard, we will compare each fabric and be able to choose a light, a medium, and a dark, relatively easily. This method eliminates the effect of color when determining value.

Note that each section is numbered, from 1 to 5. The range can be extended with white as 0, and black as 6. Compare a fabric that you are considering by placing it under all of the sections. Determine which is the closest fit, squinting if needed, and noting the number in your head or on paper. If it is not obvious which gray section the fabric matches, decide which sections that it does not match. By process of elimination, the value can be determined.

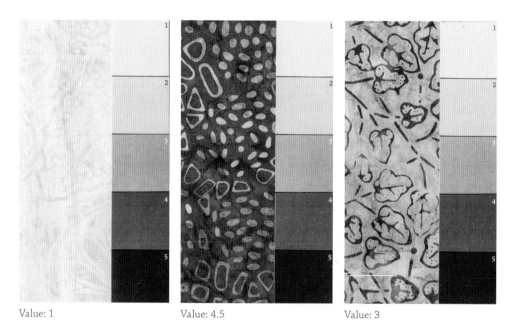

Value: 1   Value: 4.5   Value: 3

Marci finds it is easiest to find a grouping by gathering the light and dark first. Make them as far apart as can be found. Note their value number. Find a medium half way between these to get a nice even distribution. A combination of 0–3–6 will be the strongest contrast. Not every block and quilt needs this definitive style. A 1–3–5 grouping will work very well. Sara mentions in her value chart exercise on page 15 a lighter block and a darker block. These would be combinations like 1–2–3 and 4–5–6. The more evenly spaced the values are, the more obvious the 3-D illusion is.

Play with the grayscale. Have fun finding fabrics that work. If you are struggling to find a perfect medium in a particular color, don't stress. Pick the best that you can from what you have available as Marci did in her first tumbling blocks quilt, page 11. As Sara noted, the stronger value groups will carry the lesser ones. Enjoy this quick start method to learning value!

Advice for Cutting, Piecing, Pressing, and Sewing Order

There are 13 different hexagonal blocks that are interchangeable when you select the same block size (9″, 7″, or 5″), as they fit into the same space in the same way. You can make a project with all one block or mix it up using a wide variety.

We show each block first minus some seams to reinforce the design. Seams are shown between shapes of different values but not always between shapes of the same value. The construction diagrams include all the seams.

We have presented two different methods for cutting and piecing: You can individually cut the shapes using templates or rotary cutting for a scrappy/painterly look or you can choose to strip piece the blocks for faster production and a more controlled look.

Here are some general instructions that will make the finished product more successful.

CUTTING

There are three basic shapes used throughout these blocks. You can use the patterns on pages 78–83 to make templates for the shapes, or you can use a Clearview Triangle 60° ruler or Clearview Triangle Super 60° ruler. If you have one of the rulers, you may already know how to cut these shapes. Shown here is an overview for cutting each of them. If needed, use the detailed instructions on pages 76–77 until you are familiar with the steps. Then use this overview as a quick reference.

To make piecing easier and faster, Marci trims the 60° corners (marked in green on the shape's outline) using Corner Cut 60. Sara keeps the corners intact for alignment and then trims them if they are bulky or shadowing through the piecework.

Why we each choose what we do is described in the next few paragraphs. We mention this now, with cutting, because if you are going to trim corners, this is the time to do it, before they are picked up from the cutting mat.

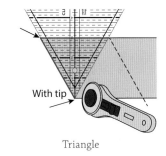

With tip

Triangle

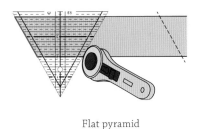

Flat pyramid

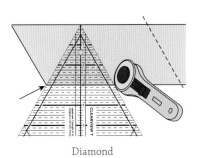

Diamond

OR

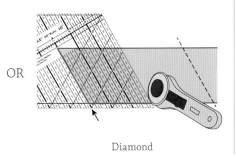

Diamond

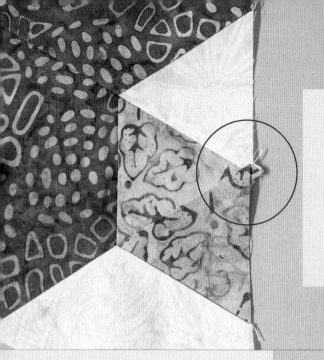

PIECING

For easy construction of the quilt, all of the hexagonal blocks are left as half blocks. This way inset seams are avoided. Each of the block instructions has a reminder to leave the block in halves.

When sewing the wedges together to make the half block, there should be ¼″ beyond where the triangles come together for the seam allowance. The seams should look something like this example.

PRESSING

Marci likes to figure out ahead of time and press so that seams are in opposing directions. Throughout the block piecing, pressing directions are indicated with arrowheads. When strip piecing these designs, light, medium, and dark strips are all sewn together. Following the general rule of pressing to the dark results in seams quite often going the same direction. By selecting the light-dark combination to press to the dark, the one most likely to shadow, the remaining combinations should press to the lighter of the two. To sum it up:

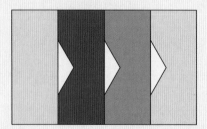

Light ⟶ Dark ⟶ Medium ⟶ Light

Sara is more casual about the seams, twisting one as necessary to eliminate bulk and to match the seams. She also controls them when shadowing might be an issue.

SEWING ORDER

Quite often the block is pieced together from 6 wedges. Sara and Marci each have their favorite way to piece and press the blocks.

Sara leaves the 60° points on the shapes to use them for alignment when the wedges come together. When she joins the wedges, she sews one wedge on and finger presses the seam away from the center. Then she adds the other wedge. She finger presses the second seam away from the center as well.

Both sides of the hexagon are made this way.

Sara aligns the tips of the fabric in the middle. She pins the points of the design together and sews. She trims the tips only if they will show through a light fabric.

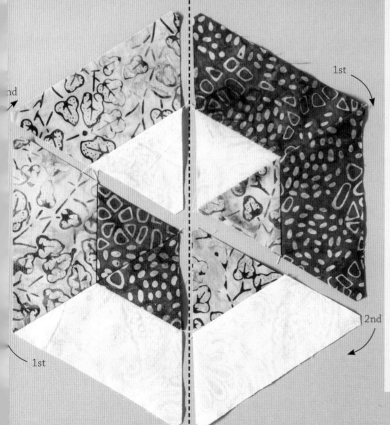

Marci trims the 60° points when the shapes are initially cut using the Corner Cut 60 because she finds it faster sewing at the machine. Then she sews and presses in a direction that results in locking or nesting seams, eliminating pinning. She sews the halves and presses in a clockwise order (counterclockwise when viewed from the wrong side). For the right half, she sews the top two wedges and presses the seam down; then she adds the third wedge and presses the seam down.

The left half starts with sewing the bottom two wedges and pressing up. Then Marci joins the third wedge and presses the seam up. When the two halves eventually come together, the seams will lock in place easily. If desired, this final seam can be manipulated so that fabric spins and flattens out for minimal bulk.

Once the blocks have been made, refer to Assembling the Quilt on page 47 for all the information needed to complete the project.

Blocks In Three Sizes

These designs have so many possibilities from intriguing wall hangings to quick kid quilts to an impressive king size quilt. The blocks in the book are provided in three different sizes: 9″, 7″, and 5″. Each size gives a totally different look. Compare the similar size of quilt made with the three sizes of blocks. You can see the openness of the 9″ blocks compared to the density of a medium-size 7″ block and the more challenging size of 5″.

Each of the block charts includes cutting for the three sizes, color coded so you can easily find the right block size for your project. The blue column is for 9″ blocks; the green column is for 7″ blocks; and yellow denotes the 5″ blocks.

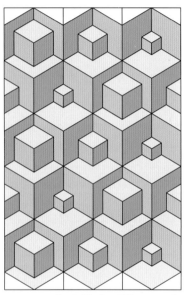

Honeycomb Waffle, Bit O'Honey, and Honey Store, 9" block, 3 × 5 blocks, 27" x 42"

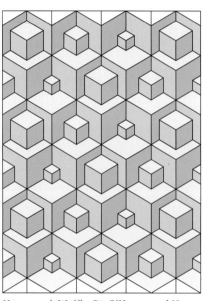

Honeycomb Waffle, Bit O'Honey, and Honey Store, 7" block, 4 × 6 blocks, 28" x 38"

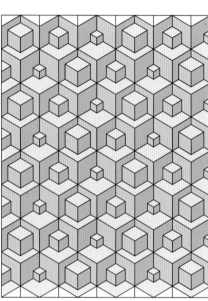

Honeycomb Waffle, Bit O'Honey, and Honey Store, 5" block, 5½ × 8 blocks, 27½" x 36"

The Blocks
A Baker's Dozen

HONEYCOMB WAFFLE
Page 22, Strip Piecing Page 23

ARCHES
Page 24, Strip Piecing Page 26

ASTEROID
Page 25, Strip Piecing Page 26

BIT O' HONEY
Page 27, Strip Piecing Page 29

HONEY STORE
Page 28, Strip Piecing Page 29

3 CUBES
Page 30, Strip Piecing Page 33

TOSS UP
Page 31, Strip Piecing Page 33

SUGAR CUBE
Page 32, Strip Piecing Page 33

HOLLOW CUBE CLASSIC
Page 35, Strip Piecing Page 38

PEEK-A-BOO
Page 36, Strip Piecing Page 39

I-SEE-YOU
Page 37, Strip Piecing Page 39

BIG BOX
Page 42, Strip Cutting Page 42

HOLE-IN-ONE
Page 43, Strip Piecing Page 45

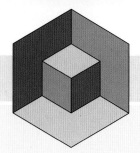

HONEYCOMB WAFFLE

An original from Sara's books on 3-D designs, this is one of the most popular blocks. And for good reason! It is the easiest block, simple enough for a confident beginner.

Qty	Value	Shape	Cut size for 9″ blocks	Cut size for 7″ blocks	Cut size for 5″ blocks
PIECES FOR ONE HONEYCOMB WAFFLE BLOCK					
2	Light	Triangles	3″	2½″	2″
2	Medium	Triangles	3″	2½″	2″
2	Dark	Triangles	3″	2½″	2″
2	Light	Flat Pyramids	5¼″ from 2¾″ strip	4¼″ from 2¼″ strip	3¼″ from 1¾″ strip
2	Medium	Flat Pyramids	5¼″ from 2¾″ strip	4¼″ from 2¼″ strip	3¼″ from 1¾″ strip
2	Dark	Flat Pyramids	5¼″ from 2¾″ strip	4¼″ from 2¼″ strip	3¼″ from 1¾″ strip

For the selected block, cut the individual shapes listed using cutting instructions on pages 76–77 or templates on pages 78–83.

Position and sew the shapes as shown. Press as indicated.

Arrange the wedges as shown. Sew as indicated to make half blocks, selecting a pressing option from pages 18–19. Do not sew the center seam.

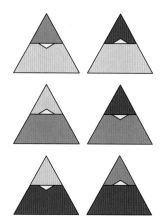

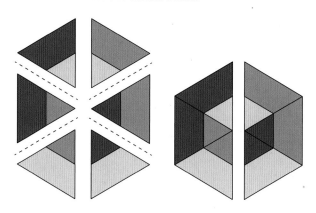

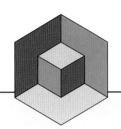
Qty	Value	Shape		Cut size for 9″ blocks (Qty 6)	Cut size for 7″ blocks (Qty 8)	Cut size for 5″ blocks (Qty 10)
2	Light	Strips		2¾″	2¼″	1¾″
2	Medium	Strips		2¾″	2¼″	1¾″
2	Dark	Strips		2¾″	2¼″	1¾″
		Triangle		5¼″	4¼″	3¼″

For the selected block, cut the strips listed in the table. The quantity of blocks from strips that are full width of fabric is listed with the block size. Sew lengthwise into 3 strip sets: light-medium, light-dark, medium-dark. Press as shown.

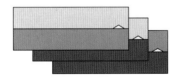

From the strip sets, cut the listed triangle size, without the ¼″ tip. This yields two different pieced triangles from each strip set.

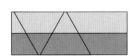

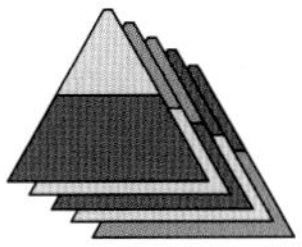

Arrange the wedges as shown. Sew as indicated to make half blocks, selecting a pressing option from pages 18–19. Do not sew the center seam.

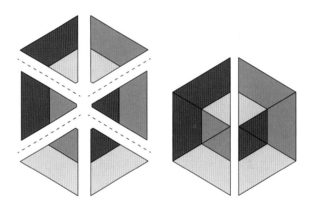

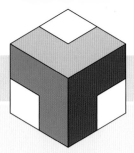

ARCHES

This variation of Sara's Downtown pattern from her 3-D illusion books has been simplified to create a whole new design. Again, this block offers success, especially to the confident beginner.

			PIECES FOR ONE ARCHES BLOCK		
Qty	Value	Shape	Cut size for 9″ blocks	Cut size for 7″ blocks	Cut size for 5″ blocks
6	Bkgd	Triangles	3″	2½″	2″
2	Light	Flat Pyramids	5¼″ from 2¾″ strip	4¼″ from 2¼″ strip	3¼″ from 1¾″ strip
2	Medium	Flat Pyramids	5¼″ from 2¾″ strip	4¼″ from 2¼″ strip	3¼″ from 1¾″ strip
2	Dark	Flat Pyramids	5¼″ from 2¾″ strip	4¼″ from 2¼″ strip	3¼″ from 1¾″ strip

For the selected block, cut the individual shapes listed using cutting instructions on pages 76–77 or templates on pages 78–83.

Position and sew the shapes as shown. Press as indicated.

Arrange the wedges as shown, alternating the direction of pressed seams, toward the background, away from the background, toward the background, and so forth. Sew as indicated to make half blocks, selecting a pressing option from pages 18–19. Do not sew the center seam.

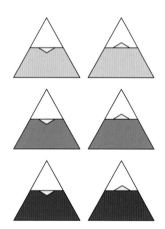

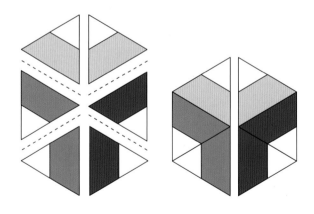

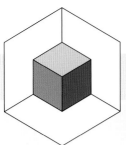

ASTEROID

Create this design from individual pieces or explore the options when strip pieced in conjunction with the Arches block. A fun block to use in a multi-block design and another block for the confident beginner.

PIECES FOR ONE ASTEROID BLOCK					
Qty	Value	Shape	Cut size for 9″ blocks	Cut size for 7″ blocks	Cut size for 5″ blocks
2	Light	Triangles	3″	2½″	2″
2	Medium	Triangles	3″	2½″	2″
2	Dark	Triangles	3″	2½″	2″
6	Bkgd	Flat Pyramids	5¼″ from 2¾″ strip	4¼″ from 2¼″ strip	3¼″ from 1¾″ strip

For the selected block, cut the individual shapes listed, using cutting instructions on pages 76–77 or templates on pages 78–83.

Position and sew the shapes as shown. Press as indicated.

Arrange the wedges as shown, alternating the direction of pressed seams, toward the background, away from the background, toward the background, and so forth. Sew as indicated to make half blocks, selecting a pressing option from pages 18–19. Do not sew the center seam.

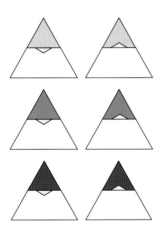

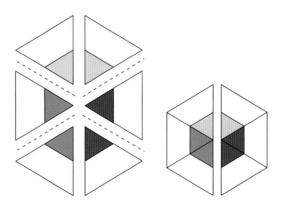

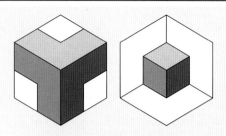

These two blocks are perfect for strip piecing at the same time without wasting fabric. Make the blocks and put them together into one quilt or make even more blocks and get two quilts, one of each block design.

STRIP PIECING FOR ARCHES AND ASTEROID					
Qty	Value	Shape		Cut size for 9″ blocks (Qty 3 each)	Cut size for 7″ blocks (Qty 4 each)	Cut size for 5″ blocks (Qty 5 each)

Qty	Value	Shape		Cut size for 9″ blocks (Qty 3 each)	Cut size for 7″ blocks (Qty 4 each)	Cut size for 5″ blocks (Qty 5 each)
1	Light	Strip		2¾″	2¼″	1¾″
1	Medium	Strip		2¾″	2¼″	1¾″
1	Dark	Strip		2¾″	2¼″	1¾″
3	Bkgd	Strips		2¾″	2¼″	1¾″
		Triangle		5¼″	4¼″	3¼″

For the blocks, cut the strips listed in the table. The quantity of blocks from strips that are full width of fabric is listed with the block size. Sew lengthwise into 3 strip sets: background-light, background-medium, background-dark. Press half of each strip set toward the background and the other half toward the light, medium, and dark fabric.

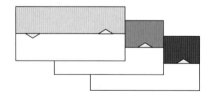

From the strip sets, cut the listed triangle size, without the ¼″ tip. This yields two different pieced triangles from each strip set. Those with the background fabric at the tip will make Arches blocks and those with the background fabric at the base will make Asteroid blocks.

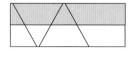

Arches   Asteroid

Arrange the wedges as shown, alternating the direction of pressed seams, toward the background, away from the background, toward the background, and so forth. Sew as indicated to make half blocks, selecting a pressing option from pages 18–19. Do not sew the center seam.

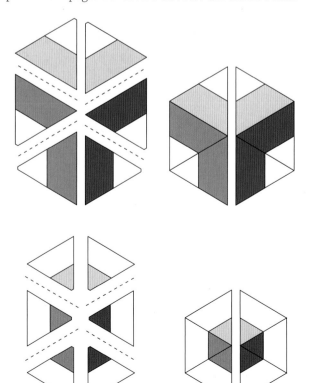

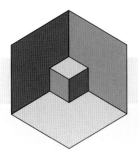

BIT O' HONEY

*Based on the original from Sara's book of building block quilts,
this Honeycomb block variation has just a taste of the 3-D design.
Great for a confident beginner, especially when strip pieced in
conjunction with Honey Store block, page 28.*

Qty	Value	Shape		Cut size for 9″ blocks	Cut size for 7″ blocks	Cut size for 5″ blocks
PIECES FOR ONE BIT O' HONEY BLOCK						
2	Light	Triangles		2¼″	2″	1¾″
2	Medium	Triangles		2¼″	2″	1¾″
2	Dark	Triangles		2¼″	2″	1¾″
2	Light	Flat Pyramids		5¼″ from 3½″ strip	4¼″ from 2¾″ strip	3¼″ from 2″
2	Medium	Flat Pyramids		5¼″ from 3½″ strip	4¼″ from 2¾″ strip	3¼″ from 2″
2	Dark	Flat Pyramids		5¼″ from 3½″ strip	4¼″ from 2¾″ strip	3¼″ from 2″

For the selected block, cut the individual shapes listed, using cutting instructions on pages 76–77 or templates on pages 78–83.

Position and sew the shapes as shown. Press as indicated.

Arrange the wedges as shown. Sew as indicated to make half blocks, selecting a pressing option from pages 18–19. Do not sew the center seam.

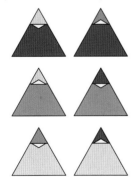

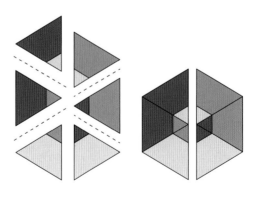

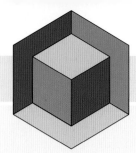

HONEY STORE

Emphasizing the cube inside the block makes this a true standout design. This block is simple enough for even a confident beginner, especially when strip pieced in conjunction with the Bit O' Honey block, page 27.

	PIECES FOR ONE HONEY STORE BLOCK				
Qty	Value	Shape	Cut size for 9″ blocks	Cut size for 7″ blocks	Cut size for 5″ blocks
2	Light	Triangles	3¾″	3″	2¼″
2	Medium	Triangles	3¾″	3″	2¼″
2	Dark	Triangles	3¾″	3″	2¼″
2	Light	Flat Pyramids	5¼″ from 2″ strip	4¼″ from 1¾″ strip	3¼″ from 1½″ strip
2	Medium	Flat Pyramids	5¼″ from 2″ strip	4¼″ from 1¾″ strip	3¼″ from 1½″ strip
2	Dark	Flat Pyramids	5¼″ from 2″ strip	4¼″ from 1¾″ strip	3¼″ from 1½″ strip

For the selected block, cut the individual shapes, using cutting instructions on pages 76–77 or templates on pages 78–83.

Position and sew the shapes as shown. Press as indicated.

Arrange the wedges as shown. Sew as indicated to make half blocks, selecting a pressing option from pages 18–19. Do not sew the center seam.

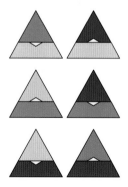

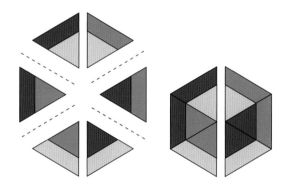

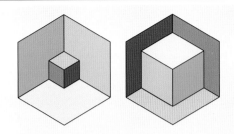

These two blocks are cut from the same strip set. A fun challenge is to make the inner block a different color than the outer block. To do this, select a light, medium, and dark for the narrow strips and another light, medium, and dark in another color for the wide strips.

			STRIP PIECING FOR BIT O' HONEY AND HONEY STORE		
Qty	Value	Shape	Cut size for 9˝ blocks (Qty 3 each)	Cut size for 7˝ blocks (Qty 4 each)	Cut size for 5˝ blocks (Qty 5 each)
2	Light	Strips	2˝	1¾˝	1½˝
2	Medium	Strips	2˝	1¾˝	1½˝
2	Dark	Strips	2'	1¾˝	1½˝
2	Light	Strips	3½˝	2¾˝	2˝
2	Medium	Strips	3½˝	2¾˝	2˝
2	Dark	Strips	3½˝	2¾˝	2˝
		Triangle	5¼˝	4¼˝	3¼˝

For the blocks, cut the strips listed in the table. The quantity of blocks from strips that are full width of fabric is listed with the block size. Sew lengthwise into 6 strip sets, each with 1 narrow strip and 1 wide strip. Use the diagram to place the values of the narrow and wide strips: light-medium, light-dark, medium-dark, medium-light, dark-light, dark-medium. Press as shown.

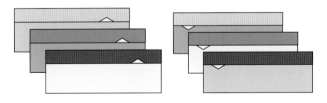

From the strip sets, cut the listed triangle size, without the ¼˝ tip.

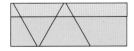

This yields two different pieced triangles from each strip set. Those with the wide strip at the base will make Bit O' Honey blocks. Those with the narrow strip at the base will make Honey Store blocks.

Arrange the wedges as shown. Sew as indicated to make half blocks, selecting a pressing option from pages 18–19. Do not sew the center seam.

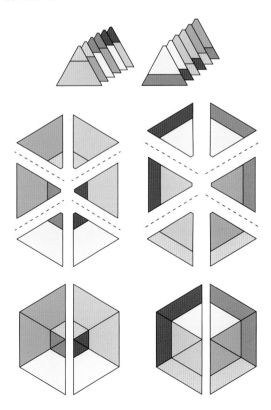

29

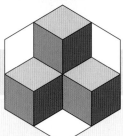

3 CUBES

This block brings back memories of playing with blocks as a child (or watching grandchildren do the same.) Simple and elegant in piecing and finished design, this block works great with many of the other blocks.

		PIECES FOR ONE 3 CUBES BLOCK			
Qty	Value	Shape	Cut size for 9″ blocks	Cut size for 7″ blocks	Cut size for 5″ blocks
6	Light	Triangles	3″	2½″	2″
3	Medium	Diamonds	2¾″	2¼″	1¾″
3	Dark	Diamonds	2¾″	2¼″	1¾″
2	Bkgd	Triangles	3″	2½″	2″
2	Bkgd	Diamonds	2¾″	2¼″	1¾″

For the selected block, cut the individual shapes listed, using cutting instructions on pages 76–77 or templates on pages 78–83.

Position and sew the shapes to make 3 left half cubes and 3 right half cubes. Press as indicated.

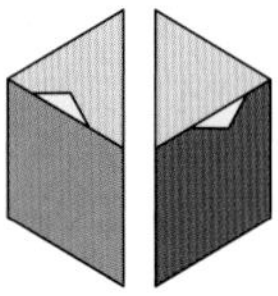

Arrange the left and right half cubes and background pieces into four columns as shown. Sew and press as indicated to make half blocks. Do not sew the center seam.

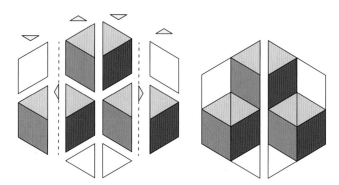

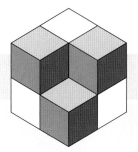

TOSS UP

Toss the 3 cubes in the air and see where they land. The top two appear to be behind the single cube. As simple as 3 Cubes, this is also a block that works well with many of the other blocks.

PIECES FOR ONE TOSS UP BLOCK

Qty	Value	Shape		Cut size for 9″ blocks	Cut size for 7″ blocks	Cut size for 5″ blocks
6	Light	Triangles		3″	2½″	2″
3	Medium	Diamonds		2¾″	2¼″	1¾″
3	Dark	Diamonds		2¾″	2¼″	1¾″
2	Bkgd	Triangles		3″	2½″	2″
2	Bkgd	Diamonds		2¾″	2¼″	1¾″

For the selected block, cut the individual shapes listed, using cutting instructions on pages 76–77 or templates on pages 78–83.

Make 3 left half cubes and 3 right half cubes. Press as indicated.

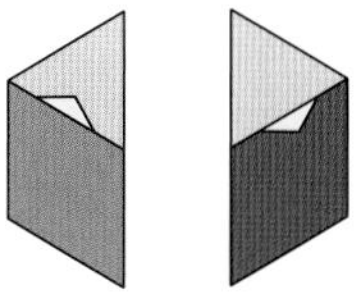

Arrange left and right half cubes and background pieces into four columns as shown.

Sew and press as indicated to make half blocks. Do not sew the center seam.

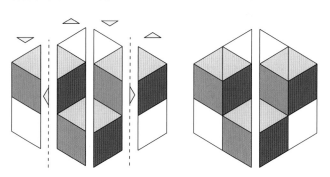

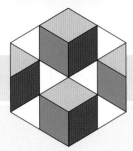

SUGAR CUBE

Reposition the blocks and now the entire quilt can be covered with sugar cubes. Since this block has only half cubes on the edges, it may or may not work with other designs as expected. Play with it and see what sweet treat can be had.

		PIECES FOR ONE SUGAR CUBE BLOCK			
Qty	Value	Shape	Cut size for 9″ blocks	Cut size for 7″ blocks	Cut size for 5″ blocks
6	Light	Triangles	3″	2½″	2″
3	Medium	Diamonds	2¾″	2¼″	1¾″
3	Dark	Diamonds	2¾″	2¼″	1¾″
6	Bkgd	Triangles	3″	2½″	2″

For the selected block, cut the individual shapes listed, using cutting instructions on pages 76–77 or templates on pages 78–83.

Make 3 left half cubes and 3 right half cubes. Press as indicated.

Sew a triangle to the side of each half cube as shown. Press as indicated.

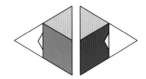

Arrange left and right half cubes units as shown. Sew as indicated to make half blocks, selecting a pressing option from pages 18–19. Do not sew the center seam.

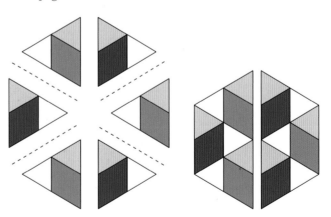

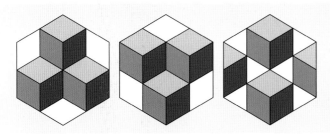

The cubes in these blocks can be strip pieced and then combined with background pieces to make the process quick. Refer to the cutting and piecing of the 3 Cube, Toss Up, and Sugar Cube blocks for the size and number of background pieces required.

			STRIP PIECING FOR CUBE BLOCKS		
Qty	Value	Shape	Cut size for 9″ blocks (Qty 8 blocks, 24 cubes)	Cut size for 7″ blocks (Qty 9 blocks, 28 cubes)	Cut size for 5″ blocks (Qty 12 blocks, 38 cubes)
2	Light	Strips	3¼″	2¾″	2¼″
2	Medium	Strips	2¾″	2¼″	1¾″
2	Dark	Strips	2¾″	2¼″	1¾″
2	Bkgd	Strips*	2¾″	2¼″	1¾″″
		Slice width	2¾″	2¼″	1¾″″

* Triangles cut without the tip

For the cubes, cut strips listed in the table. The quantity of blocks and cubes from strips that are full width of fabric is listed with the block size. Sew lengthwise into 2 strip sets: medium-light-medium and dark-light-dark. Press as indicated.

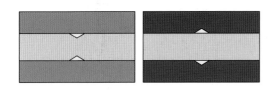

From the medium-light-medium strip set, cut left half cubes as follows:

1. Place the triangle at the right end of the strip set with point up and ruler edge at the right end of the upper seam. Match ruler lines with seams. Cut along the right edge of the triangle.

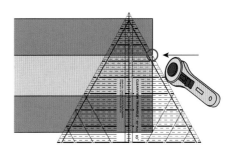

2. Turn the angled end of the strip set to the left.

Using the slice-width dimension in the chart, cut slices by aligning the appropriate ruler line along the angled end and a horizontal line along the seam (best) or the strip-set edge (OK).

After a few cuts, if the ruler lines cannot be aligned to the fabric, re-trim the angle as in Step 1. Refer to the diagram to see when one last half-cube can be cut.

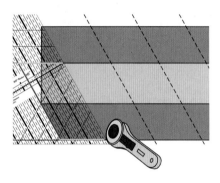

3. Cut each slice into two left half cubes as follows:

With the slice angling to the left, place any ruler line along the upper seam. Slide the ruler along the seam until the ruler edge is at the right end of the seam. The ruler edge should also line up with the left end of the bottom seam. Cut. Check the accuracy by comparing with the Actual Size Shape on page 78.

TIP If the points are not aligned, do not turn the ruler point to point, rather slide along the seam and split the variance between the end points. Basically, hide it in the seam allowance... part of the magic!

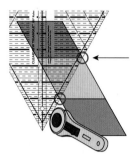

From the dark-light-dark strip set, cut right half cubes as follows:

1. Place the triangle at the right end of the strip set with the point down and ruler edge at the right end of the lower seam. Match ruler lines with seams. Cut along the right edge of the triangle.

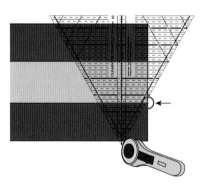

2. Turn the angled end of the strip set to the left.

Using the slice-width dimension in the chart, cut slices by aligning the appropriate ruler line along the angled end and a horizontal line along the seam (best) or the strip-set edge (OK).

After a few cuts, if the ruler lines cannot be aligned to the fabric, re-trim the angle as in Step 1. Refer to the diagram to see when one last half cube can be cut.

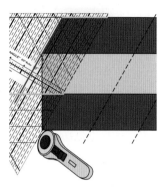

3. Cut each slice into two right half cubes as follows:

With the slice angling to the right, place any ruler line along the lower seam. Slide the ruler along the seam until the ruler edge is at the right end of the seam. The ruler edge should also line up with the left end of the top seam. Cut. Check the accuracy by comparing with the Actual Size Shape on page 78.

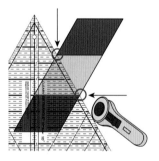

Refer to the cutting and piecing of the 3 Cube, Toss Up, and Sugar Cube blocks for the size and number of background pieces required.

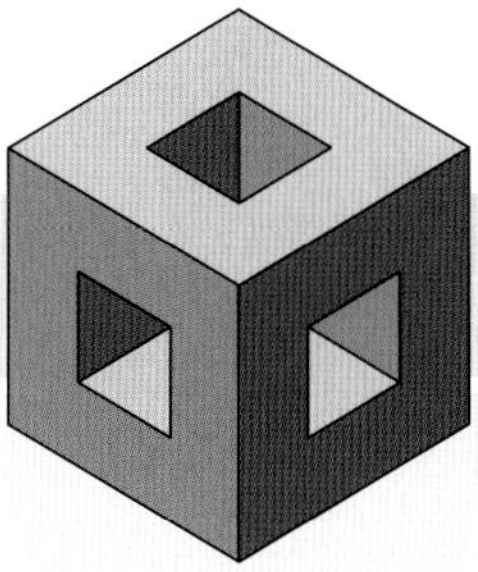

HOLLOW CUBE CLASSIC

Hollow Cube is one of Sara's classic designs for which she is well known. With this book, we are adding a new view: The "windows" can be smaller or larger than what we call classic. The size of the window is determined by the width of the strips. Wide strips give a smaller window. We have called this block Peek-A-Boo. Narrow strips give a larger window, appropriately named I-See-You. With this in mind, it is a great design for an I Spy quilt. Conversational prints with things like cars, flowers, bumblebees, etc., can be used for the triangle windows. The game is to find the items in the windows. Mix up the window sizes all in one quilt for an even more intriguing design, like Transitions, page 62.

PIECES FOR ONE HOLLOW CUBE BLOCK

Qty	Value	Shape	Cut size for 9″ blocks	Cut size for 7″ blocks	Cut size for 5″ blocks
2	Light	Triangles	2¾″	2¼″	1¾″
2	Medium	Triangles	2¾″	2¼″	1¾″
2	Dark	Triangles	2¾″	2¼″	1¾″
2	Light	Flat Pyramids	5¼″ from 1¾″ strip	4¼″ from 1½″ strip	3¼″ from 1¼″ strip
2	Light	Flat Pyramids	4″ from 1¾″ strip	3¼″ from 1½″ strip	2½″ from 1¼″ strip
2	Medium	Flat Pyramids	5¼″ from 1¾″ strip	4¼″ from 1½″ strip	3¼″ from 1¼″ strip
2	Medium	Flat Pyramids	4″ from 1¾″ strip	3¼″ from 1½″ strip	2½″ from 1¼″ strip
2	Dark	Flat Pyramids	5¼″ from 1¾″ strip	4¼″ from 1½″ strip	3¼″ from 1¼″ strip
2	Dark	Flat Pyramids	4″ from 1¾″ strip	3¼″ from 1½″ strip	2½″ from 1¼″ strip

For the selected block, cut the individual shapes listed, using cutting instructions on pages 76–77 or templates on pages 78–83.

Position and sew the shapes as shown. Press as indicated.

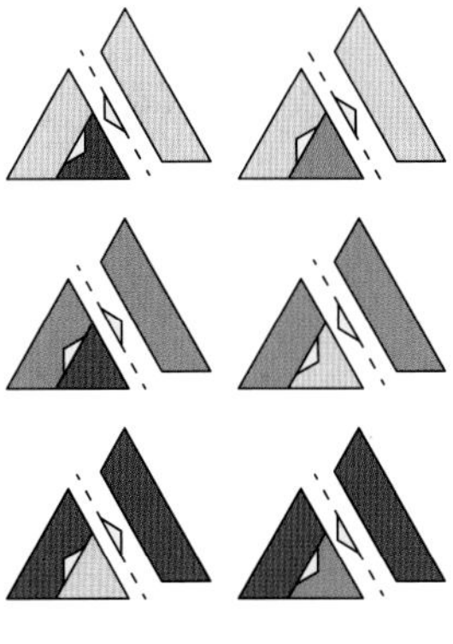

Arrange the wedges as shown. Sew as indicated to make half blocks, selecting a pressing option from pages 18–19. Do not sew the center seam.

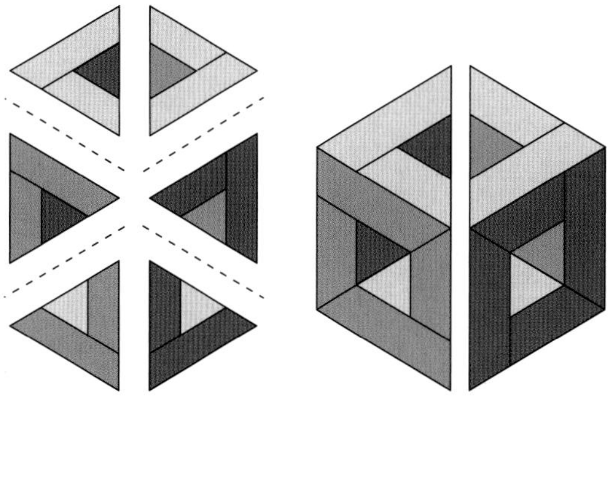

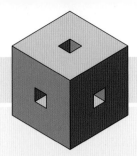

PEEK-A-BOO

The piecing of the Peek-A-Boo block is a variation
of the classic Hollow Cube block, page 35.

Qty	Value	Shape		Cut size for 9″ blocks	Cut size for 7″ blocks	Cut size for 5″ blocks
2	Light	Triangles		1¾″	1¼″	1¼″
2	Medium	Triangles		1¾″	1¼″	1¼″
2	Dark	Triangles		1¾″	1¼″	1¼″
2	Light	Flat Pyramids		5¼″ from 2¼″ strip	4¼″ from 2″ strip	3¼″ from 1½″ strip
2	Light	Flat Pyramids		3½″ from 2¼″ strip	2¾″ from 2″ strip	2¼″ from 1½″ strip
2	Medium	Flat Pyramids		5¼″ from 2¼″ strip	4¼″ from 2″ strip	3¼″ from 1½″ strip
2	Medium	Flat Pyramids		3½″ from 2¼″ strip	2¾″ from 2″ strip	2¼″ from 1½″ strip
2	Dark	Flat Pyramids		5¼″ from 2¼″ strip	4¼″ from 2″ strip	3¼″ from 1½″ strip
2	Dark	Flat Pyramids		3½″ from 2¼″ strip	2¾″ from 2″ strip	2¼″ from 1½″ strip

PIECES FOR ONE PEEK-A-BOO BLOCK

For the selected block, cut the individual shapes, using cutting instructions on pages 76–77 or templates on pages 78–83.

Position and sew the shapes as shown. Press as indicated.

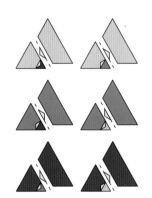

Arrange the wedges as shown. Sew as indicated to make half blocks, selecting a pressing option from pages 18–19. Do not sew the center seam.

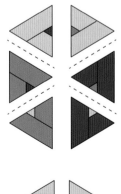

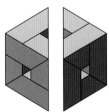

WHAT'S IN A NAME?

Sara and Marci had many discussions as to what each size variation of the Hollow Cube might be named. We did not want to go with small, medium, and large, because the medium size could be confused with the medium value. So, we decided on Classic for the middle size. Small and large are not the best descriptors for the strips because it is the width of the strip.

So, we considered:

Thin—Classic—Thick, but Marci didn't like the word "thick."

Narrow—Classic—Wide, but Sara didn't like "wide."

We went back and forth and couldn't decide on the names. Each time one of us was compromising one of the words. Somewhere along the way, we came up with the idea of names that were playful yet descriptive… and we finally did agree on "Peek-A-Boo" and "I-See-You," with the idea that in the children's game, first you can barely see what is behind the hands and then you can see everything.

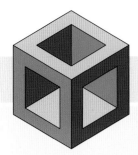

I-SEE-YOU

The piecing of the I-See-You block is the same as the classic
Hollow Cube block, page 35, of which this is a variation.

Qty	Value	Shape	Cut size for 9″ blocks	Cut size for 7″ blocks	Cut size for 5″ blocks
		PIECES FOR ONE I-SEE-YOU BLOCK			
2	Light	Triangles	3¾″	3¼″	2½″
2	Medium	Triangles	3¾″	3¼″	2½″
2	Dark	Triangles	3¾″	3¼″	2½″
2	Light	Flat Pyramids	5¼″ from 1¼″ strip	4¼″ from 1″ strip	3¼″ from ⅞″ strip
2	Light	Flat Pyramids	4½″ from 1¼″ strip	3¾″ from 1″ strip	2⅞″ from ⅞″ strip
2	Medium	Flat Pyramids	5¼″ from 1¼″ strip	4¼″ from 1″ strip	3¼″ from ⅞″ strip
2	Medium	Flat Pyramids	4½″ from 1¼″ strip	3¾″ from 1″ strip	2⅞″ from ⅞″ strip
2	Dark	Flat Pyramids	5¼″ from 1¼″ strip	4¼″ from 1″ strip	3¼″ from ⅞″ strip
2	Dark	Flat Pyramids	4½″ from 1¼″ strip	3¾″ from 1″ strip	2⅞″ from ⅞″ strip

For the selected block, cut the individual shapes, using cutting instructions on pages 76–77 or templates on pages 78–83.

Position and sew the shapes as shown. Press as indicated.

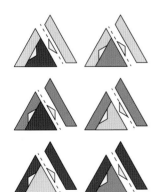

Arrange the wedges as shown. Sew as indicated to make half blocks, selecting a pressing option from pages 18–19. Do not sew the center seam.

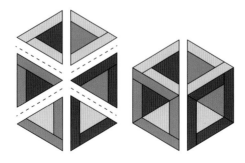

MORE VARIATION

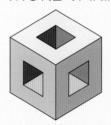

For a challenge, the color combinations for the inside and outside of the block can be different. Whether cutting individual shapes or using strip piecing, this adds a new dimension to the visual effect. Select a light, medium, and dark for the inside of the block. Cut triangles or wide strips from these. Then select a light, medium, and dark in a different color for the outside of the block. Cut Flat Pyramids or narrow strips from these.

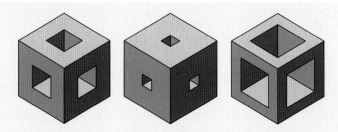

These blocks can be strip pieced individually, with the same technique, just different measurements. Use the table to select the information for the chosen block. The ruler aligns in relation to edges and seams as indicated no matter which type or size of block is being made.

Qty	Value	Shape		Cut size for 9″ blocks (Qty 9)	Cut size for 7″ blocks (Qty 10)	Cut size for 5″ blocks (Qty14)
1	Light	Inner Strip		3″	2½″	2″
1	Medium	Inner Strip		3″	2½″	2″
1	Dark	Inner Strip		3″	2½″	2″
5	Light	Outer Strips		1¾″	1½″	1¼″
5	Medium	Outer Strips		1¾″	1½″	1¼″
5	Dark	Outer Strips		1¾″	1½″	1¼″
		Slice Width		3¾″	3″	2¼″
		Triangle		4″	3¼″	2½″
2 per slice	Light	Flat Pyramids		5¼″ from 1¾″ strip	4¼″ from 1½″ strip	3¼″ from 1¼″ strip
2 per slice	Medium	Flat Pyramids		5¼″ from 1¾″ strip	4¼″ from 1½″ strip	3¼″ from 1¼″ strip
2 per slice	Dark	Flat Pyramids		5¼″ from 1¾″ strip	4¼″ from 1½″ strip	3¼″ from 1¼″ strip

Table title: **STRIP PIECING FOR HOLLOW CUBE CLASSIC BLOCKS**

STRIP PIECING FOR PEEK-A-BOO BLOCKS

Qty	Value	Shape	Cut size for 9″ blocks (Qty 10)	Cut size for 7″ blocks (Qty 12)	Cut size for 5″ blocks (Qty 16)
1	Light	Inner Strip	2″	1½″	1½″
1	Medium	Inner Strip	2″	1½″	1½″
1	Dark	Inner Strip	2″	1½″	1½″
5	Light	Outer Strips	2¼″	2″	1½″
5	Medium	Outer Strips	2¼″	2″	1½″
5	Dark	Outer Strips	2¼″	2″	1½″
		Slice Width	3¼″	2½″	2″
		Triangle	3½	2¾″	2¼″
2 per slice	Light	Flat Pyramids	5¼″ from 2¼″ strip	4¼″ from 2″ strip	3¼″ from 1½″ strip
2 per slice	Medium	Flat Pyramids	5¼″ from 2¼″ strip	4¼″ from 2″ strip	3¼″ from 1½″ strip
2 per slice	Dark	Flat Pyramids	5¼″ from 2¼″ strip	4¼″ from 2″ strip	3¼″ from 1½″ strip

STRIP PIECING FOR I-SEE-YOU BLOCKS

Qty	Value	Shape	Cut size for 9″ blocks (Qty 8)	Cut size for 7″ blocks (Qty 9)	Cut size for 5″ blocks (Qty 12)
1	Light	Inner Strip	4″	3½″	2¾″
1	Medium	Inner Strip	4″	3½″	2¾″
1	Dark	Inner Strip	4″	3½″	2¾″
5	Light	Outer Strips	1¼″	1″	⅞″
5	Medium	Outer Strips	1¼″	1″	⅞″
5	Dark	Outer Strips	1¼″	1″	⅞″
		Slice Width	4¼″	3½″	2⅝″
		Triangle	4½″	3¾″	2⅞″
2 per slice	Light	Flat Pyramids	5¼″ from 1¼″ strip	4¼″ from 1″ strip	3¼″ from ⅞″ strip
2 per slice	Medium	Flat Pyramids	5¼″ from 1¼″ strip	4¼″ from 1″ strip	3¼″ from ⅞″ strip
2 per slice	Dark	Flat Pyramids	5¼″ from 1¼″ strip	4¼″ from 1″ strip	3¼″ from ⅞″ strip

For the selected block, cut the strips listed in the table. Sew lengthwise into 3 strip sets, with the inner strip being the center strip in the strip sets: medium-light-dark, dark-medium-light, light-dark-medium. Press as indicated.

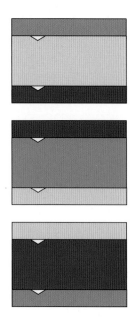

Set aside the remaining narrow strips to use for the Flat Pyramid pieces.

Cut and sew triangle units using the corresponding sizes from the table, as follows:

1. To establish a 60° angle, place a triangle ruler at the right end of the strip set with the point up. Match ruler lines with seams. Cut along the right edge of the triangle.

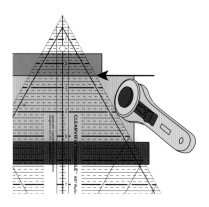

2. Turn the angled end of the strip set to the left. Cut slices, the size shown in the table, by aligning the ruler line along the angled end and a horizontal line along the seam (highlighted in green) or fabric edge (highlighted in yellow.) After a few cuts, if the ruler lines cannot be aligned, trim the angle as in Step 1.

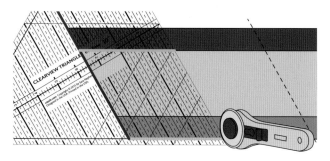

3. Cut 2 triangles from each slice, using the size listed in the table. With the slice angling to the left, place the triangle size ruler line along the upper edge, with the left edges of the ruler and slice aligned. Use the triangle size from the table.

The tip of the ruler should be at the seam (or close to it). Note that the triangle should be missing a tip at the upper right corner. These are designated by the circles.

Turn the slice and cut the other triangle in the same way. Expect a scrap of fabric to be left over.

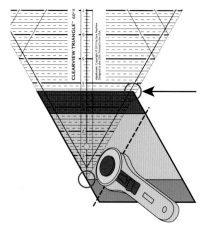

From the remaining narrow strips, cut Flat Pyramids as listed in the table. Position and sew these on one side of the triangle units. Press as shown.

Arrange the wedges as shown. Sew as indicated to make half blocks, selecting a pressing option from pages 18–19. Do not sew the center seam.

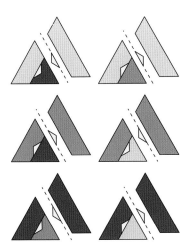

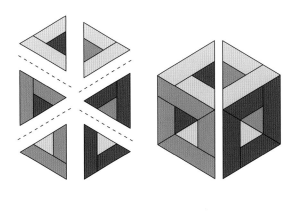

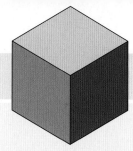

BIG BOX

One large cube is great for resting the eyes with many smaller shapes. This works well with most of the other blocks.

PIECES FOR ONE BIG BOX BLOCK

Qty	Value	Shape		Cut size for 9″ blocks	Cut size for 7″ blocks	Cut size for 5″ blocks
2	Light	Triangles		5¼″	4¼″	3¼″
1	Medium	Diamond		5″	4″	3″
1	Dark	Diamond		5″	4″	3″

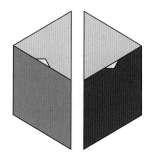

For the selected block, cut the individual shapes, using cutting instructions on pages 76–77 or templates on pages 78–83.

Position and sew the shapes as shown to make a left half block and a right half block. Press as indicated. Do not sew the center seam.

STRIP CUTTING FOR BIG BOX

Marci usually does not use strip piecing to make the Big Box blocks because of the large size of the pieces. But you can cut the diamonds and triangles from strips. The yield from a strip for a shape is indicated on the actual size template, pages 78–83.

CUTTING BIG BOX PIECES FROM STRIPS

	Value	Shape		Cut size for 9″ blocks	Cut size for 7″ blocks	Cut size for 5″ blocks
	Light	Triangles		5¼″	4¼″	3¼″
Qty	Medium	Diamond		5″	4″	3″
	Dark	Diamond		5″	4″	3″

HOLE-IN-ONE

Hole-In-One (Top)

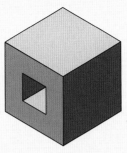

Hole-In-One (Left)

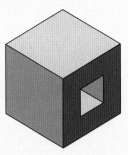

Hole-In-One (Right)

Combine the Big Box with the Hollow Cube designs and what do you have? A hole in one! One side of the cube, that is. The hole can be placed on the top, bottom left, or bottom right side of the cube. Pick the side and then pick the pieces. Realize that the top always needs to remain split into left and right triangles.

For the selected block, cut the individual shapes, using cutting instructions on pages 76–77 or templates on pages 78–83.

PIECES FOR ONE HOLE-IN-ONE BLOCK (TOP)

Qty	Value	Shape	Cut size for 9″ blocks	Cut size for 7″ blocks	Cut size for 5″ blocks
2	Light	Flat Pyramids	5¼″ from 1¾″ Strip	4¼″ from 1½″ Strip	3¼″ from 1¼″ Strip
2	Light	Flat Pyramids	4″ from 1¾″ Strip	3¼″ from 1½″ Strip	2½″ from 1¼″ Strip
1	Medium	Triangle	2¾″	2¼″	1¾″
1	Dark	Triangle	2¾″	2¼″	1¾″
1	Medium	Diamond	5″	4″	3″
1	Dark	Diamond	5″	4″	3″

Position and sew the shapes as shown. Press as indicated.

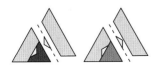

Arrange the triangle units and diamonds as shown. Sew and press as indicated to make half blocks. Do not sew the center seam.

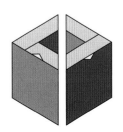

PIECES FOR ONE HOLE-IN-ONE BLOCK (LEFT)

Qty	Value	Shape	Cut size for 9″ blocks	Cut size for 7″ blocks	Cut size for 5″ blocks
2	Medium	Flat Pyramids	5¼″ from 1¾″ Strip	4¼″ from 1½″ Strip	3¼″ from 1¼″ Strip
2	Medium	Flat Pyramids	4″ from 1¾″ Strip	3¼″ from 1½″ Strip	2½″ from 1¼″ Strip
1	Light	Triangle	2¾″	2¼″	1¾″
1	Dark	Triangle	2¾″	2¼″	1¾″
2	Light	Triangle	5¼″	4¼″	3¼″
1	Dark	Diamond	5″	4″	3″

Position and sew the shapes as shown. Press as indicated.

Arrange the triangle units and diamonds as shown. Sew and press as indicated to make half blocks. Do not sew the center seam.

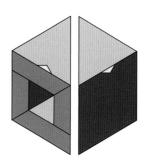

PIECES FOR ONE HOLE-IN-ONE BLOCK (RIGHT)

Qty	Value	Shape	Cut size for 9″ blocks	Cut size for 7″ blocks	Cut size for 5″ blocks
2	Dark	Flat Pyramids	5¼″ from 1¾″ Strip	4¼″ from 1½″ Strip	3¼″ from 1¼″ Strip
2	Dark	Flat Pyramids	4″ from 1¾″ Strip	3¼″ from 1½″ Strip	2½″ from 1¼″ Strip
1	Light	Triangle	2¾″	2¼″	1¾″
1	Medium	Triangle	2¾″	2¼″	1¾″
2	Light	Triangle	5¼″	4¼″	3¼″
1	Medium	Diamond	5″	4″	3″

Position and sew the shapes as shown. Press as indicated.

Arrange the triangle units and diamonds as shown. Sew and press as indicated to make half blocks. Do not sew the center seam.

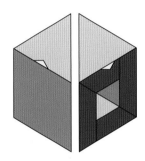

STRIP PIECING FOR HOLE-IN-ONE BLOCKS

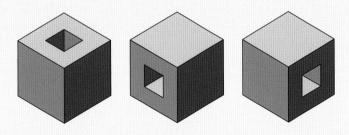

Strip piecing Hole-in-One blocks is not practical. The method of strip-piecing used for Hollow Cube Classic, page 38, would create pieces that are not used in the block. This defeats the purpose of strip-piecing.

If desired, strip piece for Hollow Cube Classic, Peek-a-Boo, or I-See-You and add in pieces from Big Box. There are a lot of options.

Assemble the Quilt Top

Ta-da! Now you have the blocks made and the magic happens. Play with the arrangement. Know that you have some options. Consider if you need some blank space, how you want to finish the edges, or if you want a completely different design with setting triangles. Here are the details to make these options happen.

BLANK SPACE

Blank space is our term for pieces of background fabric that finish the edges and emphasize the pieced blocks. The side edges can be filled in with pieced half blocks as shown in the right edge of the illustration. Or they can be filled in with blank space pieces as shown on the left edge. The half hexagon can also be used in pairs, forming a full hexagon to allow focus on the other blocks. See Hollow Cube Classic by Kathy Syring, page 66 for an example.

When using blank spaces, the sizes to cut should be as listed in the table. However, variation in cutting, sewing, and pressing methods can make your sizes different. If the size of your pieced half block is more than ¼″ different, use your piece as a template. Cutting instructions are on page 77. Leave these as half blocks.

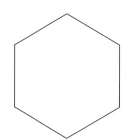

Full-Hexagon Blank Space

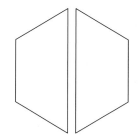

Half-Hexagon Blank Spaces

PIECES FOR ONE BLANK SPACE					
Qty	Value	Shape	Cut size for 9″ blocks	Cut size for 7″ blocks	Cut size for 5″ blocks
2	Bkgd	Flat Pyramid	9¾″ from 5″ Strip	7¾″ from 4″ Strip	5¾″ from 3″ Strip

TRIANGLE HALVES

Triangle halves are used to square off the design at the top and bottom. Notice there are left and right triangle halves. Determine how many of each are needed. Cut the appropriate number of rectangles knowing that one rectangle provides either two left or two right. See page 77 for specific cutting instructions.

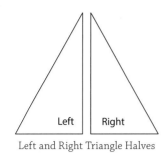

Left and Right Triangle Halves

TIP Some batiks and solids are the same on both sides, so you can just flip them over if you need the other side.

Qty	Value	Shape	Cut size for 9" blocks	Cut size for 7" blocks	Cut size for 5" blocks
TRIANGLE HALVES TO FINISH EDGES					
2	Bkgd	Rectangle	3⅜" × 5¾"	2¾" × 4¾"	2⅛" × 3¾"

SETTING TRIANGLES

For another design option, Sara added setting triangles between the blocks. Cubicle, page 56, has these as part of the design. By making half of them medium and half of them dark, the 3-D space is even larger. For instructions on how to use setting triangles, refer to the pattern instructions for Cubicle.

Qty	Value	Shape	Cut size for 9" blocks	Cut size for 7" blocks	Cut size for 5" blocks
SETTING TRIANGLES					
1	Bkgd	Triangle	5¼"	4¼"	3¼"

ASSEMBLING THE QUILT

Once the arrangement is set, sew columns of alternating left and right half blocks. Press the seams in opposing directions from column to column. Matching the left and right half blocks, sew the columns together. Press in one direction. To complete the quilt top, add pieced or plain borders, if you wish.

TIP Sometimes it can be confusing as to which way to press the seams in the next column, and a headache can appear on the horizon. To ward that off, Marci recommends not pressing until after all of the columns are sewn. Then pick up every other column at the top and every other one at the bottom. Press toward the designated end. Either lay them out again or keep them in their two stacks to sew in pairs. Either way, they are ready to sew, headache free.

The Quilt Designs

ARCHES
Page 50

BUBBLE UP
Page 52

CLIFF
Page 54

CUBICLE
Page 56

MY CLOUD
Page 58

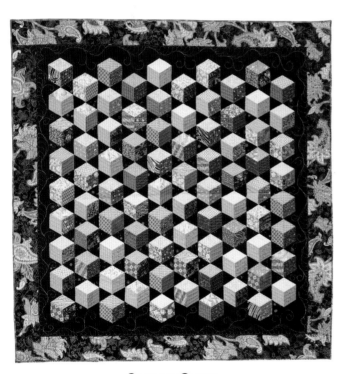

SUGAR CUBE
Page 60

TRANSITIONS
Page 62

ARCHES *by Kathy Syring*

BLOCK SIZE: 9″ • **QUILT SIZE:** 53″ × 65″
(45″ × 57¼″ without borders)

Kathy is using an interesting combination of colors in a dramatic way. Red shades toward orange, yellow shades toward gold. Blue gets closer to purple, and green is a rich avocado. Not only that, her arrangement of colors can trick your eyes, too. The colors in the arch shapes will look consistent, and then you notice a color sliding over to the next row, changing an arch into a circle, or into a Y. And, look here, the background is white! Add a white border and you see that this quilt is a very striking modern design. Notice how Kathy played with the colors, blending them so that some of the blocks are all one color, like those in the top row. Then she has multi-color blocks to create the rings as the color progresses across the quilt. Play with it and make it your own.

MATERIALS

Following your piecing preference, select yardage amounts for cutting individual shapes or for strip piecing.

Fabric Amounts for Individual Shapes

2 yards total of light

2 yards total of medium

2 yards total of dark

1¼ yards for background blocks and setting

Fabric Amounts for Strip Piecing

⅜ yd of each of light, medium, and dark in 5 color combinations (15 fabrics total)

1¼ yards background for blocks and setting

Fabric Amounts for Finishing

1 yard for border

½ yard for binding

Construction

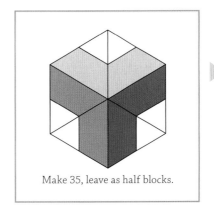

Make 35, leave as half blocks.

Make 35 Arches blocks, page 24.

NOTE If the blocks were strip pieced, there will be remaining triangles that can be put together into an Asteroid quilt. See Kathy's version of this quilt in the gallery, page 66. Or you can play with both blocks together and make something like Janet Blazekovich's *Asteroids and Arches*, page 64.

ASSEMBLY

For the triangle halves for the top and bottom edges, cut 2 strips 3⅜″ wide x WOF. Cut 10 rectangles 3⅜″ × 5¾″. Follow instructions on page 77 to cut triangle halves. Make 10 left and 10 right.

Place the blocks and triangle halves as shown or in an arrangement that is pleasing to you.

Sew the pieces into columns, making 10 columns. Press as shown. Sew the columns together, pressing seams in one direction.

Finish the quilt with borders. Cut 6 strips 4½″ × WOF. Measure, sew, and apply side borders. Measure, sew, and apply top and bottom borders.

BUBBLE UP *by Kristi Droese*

BLOCK SIZE: 9˝ • **QUILT SIZE:** 52½˝ × 69¼˝
(40½˝ × 57¼˝ without borders)

Kristi has been able to find a great selection of light, medium, and dark fabrics in each color she chose. The combination is playful and very 3-D. Mixing Hollow Cube blocks with Honeycomb Waffle blocks creates interesting shapes and intersections. Textures and solid fabrics mix well, and the bouncy visual action is surrounded and held together by triangle halves and borders of black fabric.

MATERIALS

Following your piecing preference, select yardage amounts for cutting individual shapes or for strip piecing.

Fabric Amounts for Individual Shapes

2 yards total of light

2 yards total of medium

2 yards total of dark

Fabric Amounts for Strip Piecing

⅜ yard each of light, medium, and dark in 5 colors (15 fabrics total)

Fabric Amounts for Finishing

1⅝ yards for setting and borders

½ yard for binding

Construction

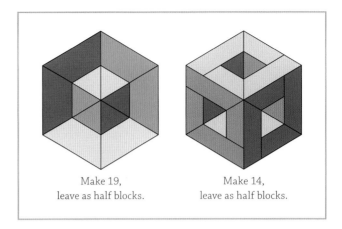

Make 19,
leave as half blocks.

Make 14,
leave as half blocks.

▷ Make 19 Honeycomb Waffle blocks, page 22. (There will be two left half blocks extra.)

▷ Make 14 Hollow Cube Classic blocks, page 35. (There will be one right half block extra.)

ASSEMBLY

For triangle halves for the top and bottom edges, cut 2 strips 3⅜″ wide x WOF. Cut 10 rectangles 3⅜″ × 5¾″. Follow instructions on page 77 to cut triangle halves. Make 9 left and 9 right.

Place the blocks and triangle halves as shown or in an arrangement that is pleasing to you.

Sew the pieces into 9 columns. Press as shown. Sew the columns together, pressing seams in one direction.

Finish the quilt with borders. Cut 6 strips 6½″ × WOF. Measure, sew, and apply side borders. Measure, sew, and apply top and bottom borders.

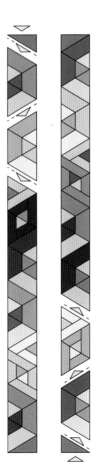

CLIFF *by Elaine Muzichuk*

BLOCK SIZE: 9˝ • **QUILT SIZE:** 61½˝ × 77˝
(49½˝ × 65˝ without borders)

This quilt is made out of flannel, so perhaps that added an extra touch of softness to the look of the quilt. Or maybe it's just some soft color choices. The Big Box block works visually with the Hollow Cube variation I-See-You, and Elaine shows us how to mix the two with some Hole-in-One blocks. Flickering light and changing perspectives flow, almost like water. A final dark border flickers a bit too.

Construction

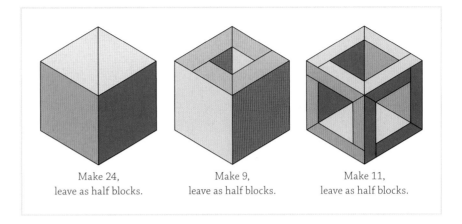

Make 24,
leave as half blocks.

Make 9,
leave as half blocks.

Make 11,
leave as half blocks.

MATERIALS

Fabric Amounts for Individual Shapes or Strip Piecing

⅜ yard each of light, medium, and dark in 6 colors (18 fabrics total)

Fabric Amounts for Finishing

⅜ yard for setting

1½ yards for borders

¾ yard for binding

▷ Make 24 Big Box blocks, page 42.

▷ Make 9 Hole-in-One (Top) blocks, page 43.

▷ Make 11 I-See-You blocks, page 37.

ASSEMBLY

For the triangle halves, cut 2 strips 3⅜″ wide x WOF. Cut 11 rectangles 3⅜″ × 5¾″. Follow instructions on page 77 to cut triangle halves. Make 10 left and 12 right.

Place the blocks and triangle halves as shown or in an arrangement that is pleasing to you.

Sew the pieces into 11 columns. Press as shown. Sew the columns together, pressing seams in one direction.

Finish the quilt with borders. Cut 7 strips 6½″ × WOF. Measure, sew, and apply side borders. Measure, sew, and apply top and bottom borders.

CUBICLE *by Alicia Sanchez*

BLOCK SIZE: 9″ • **QUILT SIZE:** 49½″ × 60¼″
(36″ × 46¾″ without borders)

This quilt encompasses a full lecture on using value to create an illusion of 3-D. As they say, "A picture is worth a thousand words." For her light fabric, Alicia has chosen a fabric close to being white, but not. And a dark fabric close to being black, but not. And her medium fabric has colors, but very subtle. Actual black, white, and gray would be bold by comparison. In this softer combination, it's easy to imagine offices or buildings at night and one person—a burglar—maybe not. The interesting corners on the borders remind one of picture holders in old-time albums with this quilt a black and white snapshot. Hang this in an office or take a nap under it. It works!

MATERIALS

Fabric Amounts for Individual Shapes or Strip Piecing

¾ yard of light for blocks and setting

1¼ yards of medium for blocks and setting

1¼ yard of dark for blocks and setting

Fabric Amounts for Finishing

¾ yard of medium for pieced border

¼ yard of dark for pieced border

¾ yard of accent for inner border and border corners

Construction

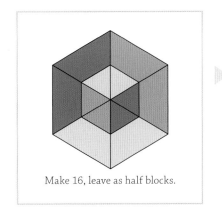

Make 16, leave as half blocks.

Make 16 Honeycomb Waffle blocks, page 22.

ASSEMBLY

From medium and dark, cut 1 strip 5¼″ × WOF from each. From each strip, cut 12 triangles 5¼″ (see page 76).

From medium and dark, cut 1 strip 5″ × WOF from each. From each strip, cut 4 diamonds 5″ (see page 77).

For triangle halves, from light, medium, and dark, cut 1 strip 3⅜″ × WOF from each.

From the light strip, cut 5 rectangles 3⅜″ × 5¾″. Follow instructions on page 77 to cut triangle halves. Make 4 right and 6 left.

From a medium strip, cut 1 rectangle 3⅜″ × 5¾″. Follow instructions on page 77 to cut triangle halves. Make 2 left.

From the dark strip, cut 2 rectangles 3⅜″ × 5¾″. Follow instructions on page 77 to cut triangle halves. Make 4 right.

Place the half blocks, diamonds, triangles, and triangle halves as shown.

Sew the pieces into 8 columns. Press as shown. Sew columns together, pressing seams in one direction. fig. A

PIECED BORDER

Measure your own piecework and modify the following lengths as necessary.

From accent fabric, cut 7 strips 2¾″ × WOF. From 2 of the strips, cut 24 squares 2¾″ × 2¾″. From the remaining strips, make the border pieces as shown in the diagram.

From medium, cut 8 strips 2¾″ × WOF. Make the border pieces as shown in the diagram.

From dark, cut 2 strips 2¾″ × WOF. Cut 20 squares 2¾″ × 2¾″. From remaining fabric, cut 4 squares 5″ × 5″. figs. B-C

For the top and bottom borders, add the squares to the medium border pieces. Join the medium and accent border pieces and sew to the quilt center. Press to the borders.

For the side borders, add the squares to the border pieces. Join the medium border pieces then add the large corner square. Join the medium and accent border pieces and sew to the quilt center. Press to the borders.

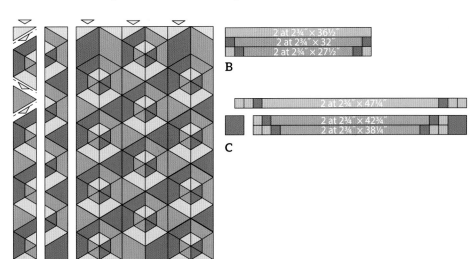

A

2 at 2¾″ × 36½″
2 at 2¾″ × 32″
2 at 2¾″ × 27½″
B

2 at 2¾″ × 47¾″
2 at 2¾″ × 42¾″
2 at 2¾″ × 38¼″
C

MY CLOUD *by Sara Nephew*

BLOCK SIZE: 9″ • **QUILT SIZE:** 39½″ × 41¾″
(31½″ × 33¾″ without borders)

Sara wanted to try more graphic fabric prints plus just play with her favorite blocks. She started with a couple of Honeycomb Waffle blocks left from another project and taped them up where they could be seen. Then she made a few Hollow Cube blocks. She dug into her scraps to make 3 Cubes and Toss Up and the project started to happen! More polka dots and stripes! When it was laid out on the floor it looked almost finished, and a few Sugar Cube blocks pulled it together. Shades of gray often work well for borders on a 3-D quilt, since it brings out the values of the design. Because of the variety of blocks and fabrics used, a general yardage amount is provided for the various values. This is a minimum and should consist of a variety of designs and values to achieve the resulting project.

Construction

MATERIALS

Fabric Amounts for Individual Shapes or Strip Piecing

½ yard total of light

½ yard total of medium

½ yard total of dark

½ yard of background for blocks and setting

Fabric Amounts for Finishing

¾ yard for border

½ yard for binding

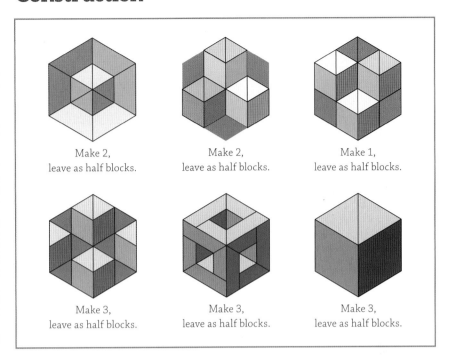

Make 2, leave as half blocks.

Make 2, leave as half blocks.

Make 1, leave as half blocks.

Make 3, leave as half blocks.

Make 3, leave as half blocks.

Make 3, leave as half blocks.

Follow the directions to make the blocks. Be sure to leave as half blocks.

▶ Make 2 Honeycomb Waffle blocks, page 22.

▶ Make 3 Sugar Cube blocks, page 32.

▶ Make 2 3 Cubes blocks, page 30.

▶ Make 3 Hollow Cube blocks, page 35.

▶ Make 1 Toss Up block, page 31.

▶ Make 3 Big Box blocks, page 42.

ASSEMBLY

For the triangle halves, cut 2 strips 3⅜″ wide x WOF. Cut 7 rectangles 3⅜″ × 5¾″. Follow instructions on page 77 to cut triangle halves. Make 8 left and 6 right.

Place the blocks and triangle halves as shown or in an arrangement that is pleasing to you.

Sew the pieces into 7 columns. Press as shown. Sew the columns together, pressing seams in one direction.

Finish the quilt with borders. Cut 5 strips 4½″ × WOF. Measure, sew, and apply the side borders. Measure, sew, and apply the top and bottom borders.

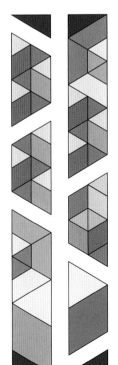

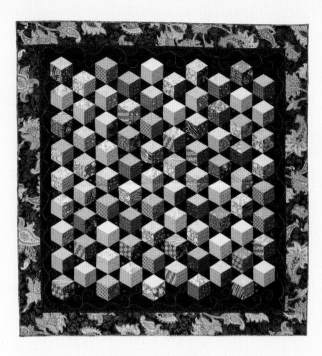

SUGAR CUBE *by Sara Nephew*

BLOCK SIZE: 9˝ • **QUILT SIZE:** 57˝ × 58¾˝
(45˝ × 46¾˝ without borders)

Making the whole quilt out of the Sugar Cube block takes only a little planning. You can choose just three fabrics, a dark, a medium, and a light, make all the blocks the same, and then it should go zip, zip, zip. But if, like Sara, you love scraps, you will need to lay out each block and aim to fit colors together where edge half blocks combine. As long as value choices are good, color can vary somewhat. Sara finished the sides with columns of half cubes and background triangles so that we see complete cubes at the edges. A black inner border separates the cubes from a flowing large print for a contrasting and pleasing finish. Choose either a scrappy color plan or a very simple plan with minimal colors which is easier to organize.

MATERIALS

Following your piecing preference, select yardage amounts for cutting individual shapes or for strip piecing.

Fabric Amounts for Individual Shapes

2 yards total of light

2 yards total of medium

2 yards total of dark

1¾ yards of background for blocks and setting

Fabric Amounts for Strip Piecing

⅜ yard each of light, medium, and dark in 6 colors (18 fabrics total)

1¾ yards of background for blocks and setting

Fabric Amounts for Finishing

½ yards for inner borders

1 yard for outer border

½ yard for binding

ASSEMBLY

Cut 33 triangles 2¾″ from background fabric.

Using the previously made half cubes and the background triangles, make 4 partial half blocks, left and 5 partial half blocks, right.

Using the previously made half cubes and the background triangles, make the side edge columns with 9 left half cubes on the left column and 8 right half cubes on the right column.

For the triangle halves, cut 2 strips 3⅜″ × WOF. Cut 8 rectangles 3⅜″ × 5¾″. Follow instructions on page 77 to cut triangle halves. Make 8 left and 8 right.

For the triangle halves for the corners, cut 2 rectangles 4⅝″ × 8″. Follow the instructions on page 77 to cut triangle halves. Make 1 left and 1 right. From the leftover triangle halves, cut 2 rectangles, 2⅛″ × 3¾″. Cut triangle halves. Make 1 left and 1 right.

Place the blocks, partial blocks, and triangle halves as shown or in an arrangement that is pleasing to you.

Sew the pieces into 9 columns. Press as shown. Sew the 9 columns and side columns together, pressing seams in one direction.

Construction

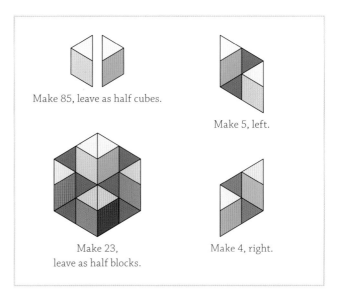

Make 85, leave as half cubes.

Make 5, left.

Make 23, leave as half blocks.

Make 4, right.

▷ Make 85 cubes, to use in the Sugar Cube blocks and in the partial blocks at the top and on the side columns, page 32.

▷ Make 23 Sugar Cube blocks, using the previously made half cubes, and leave them as half blocks. (There will be 1 half block extra.) To keep the cubes matched from block to block, make one block and use the other half of the side cubes for the next block. Gradually work across the quilt, and arrange colors as you sew the half blocks.

Finish the quilt with borders. From background fabric, cut 5 strips 2½″ × WOF. Measure, sew, and apply the side borders. Measure, sew, and apply the top and bottom borders.

From print border fabric, cut 6 strips 4½″ × WOF. Measure, sew, and apply the side borders. Measure, sew, and apply the top and bottom borders.

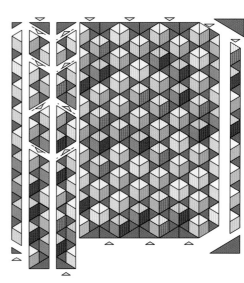

TRANSITIONS

by Marci Baker

BLOCK SIZE: 9″ • **QUILT SIZE:** 65″ × 73¼″
(54″ × 62¼″ without borders)

This looks like an amazingly complex, over-the-top quilt. But it is surprisingly simple. Marci decided to do a little math for making a Hollow Cube with thin, middle-sized, or thick walls. In this quilt, she uses all three variations. The plan starts at the bottom, with thin walls. Then middle-sized, then thick walled at the top. These Hollow Cubes are all blue inside, and gold to brick on the outside. Then she adds a row of left-right diamond walls with no openings. Easy! The next set also goes thin to thick. This time the gold and brick colors go inside, and the outsides are a rich rose. Voila! And this book gives you the measurements for strips to quick-piece these blocks, appropriately named Hollow Cube Classic, and the new Peek-A-Boo and I-See-You blocks so you can use them wherever you want.

1 yard each light, medium, and dark for colorway A (pink)

1¼ yards each light, medium, dark for colorway B (yellow)

⅝ yard each light, medium, dark for colorway C (teal)

Fabric Amounts for Finishing

1½ yards for border

⅝ yard for binding

Construction

The challenge of this quilt is being organized. To help with this, we recommend that you make a swatch card (fabric taped to a card and labeled as A, B, C, and light, medium, and dark, and refer to it while working on each block.

| Make 6 of colorway A, leave as half blocks. | Make 12, 6 of colorway A/B and 6 of colorway B/C, leave as half blocks. | Make 12, 6 of colorway A/B and 6 of colorway B/C, leave as half blocks. | Make 12, 6 of colorway A/B and 6 of colorway B/C, leave as half blocks. |

Follow the directions to make the blocks. Be sure to leave as half blocks.

▷ Make 6 Big Box, colorway A, page 42

▷ Make 6 Peek-A-Boo, colorway A/B inside, page 36

▷ Make 6 Hollow Cube Classic, colorway A/B inside, page 35

▷ Make 6 I-See-You, colorway A/B inside, page 37

▷ Make 6 Peek-A-Boo, colorway B/C inside, page 36

▷ Make 6 Hollow Cube Classic, colorway B/C inside, page 35

▷ Make 6 I-See-You, colorway B/C inside, page 37

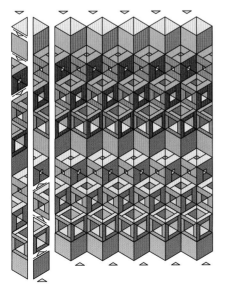

ASSEMBLY

From colorway B, medium and dark, cut 1 strip 5" x WOF from each. Cut 6 diamonds of each.

From colorway C, medium and dark, cut 1 strip 5″ × WOF from each. Cut 6 diamonds of each.

Place the half blocks and diamonds as shown or in an arrangement that is pleasing to you.

Sew the pieces into 12 columns. Press as shown. Sew the columns together, pressing seams in one direction.

Trim the blocks on the top and bottom edges to make straight edges.

Finish the quilt with borders. Cut 7 strips 6″ × WOF. Measure, sew, and apply side borders. Measure, sew, and apply top and bottom borders.

Gallery

ASTEROIDS AND ARCHES *by Janet Blazekovich*

PLAYING WITH BLOCKS *by Kate McIntyre*

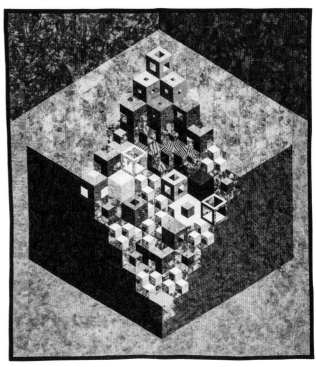

Rocket ships to the moon! There's a lot of motion in this slice of sky. A pointing arm and rows of cubes look like rockets advancing in rows. Janet chose bright colors that make a child (or a grownup) feel the fun in this action. The light background is the opposite of space (what if it were black?), but we still feel like we're floating away.

Kate took the block patterns and ran with them, using slippery-looking batiks, floral prints, even zebra stripes. Her 3-D illusion seems to be a huge cube (dark side on the left) that's opening up on one corner so you can see all the insides (notice dark sides on the left). Or are they instead piled up reaching for the sky? Lots of purple, said by some to be a quilter's favorite color.

TUMBLING BLOCKS *by Sara Nephew*

STONE CANYON *by Martha Ethridge*

Sara loves scraps so she got a chance to really dive in here. She even used some decorator fabrics. The 3 Cubes block easily produces allover Tumbling Blocks when the background corner pieces are switched to light, medium, and dark in the correct places. Color doesn't matter as long as the values are correct.

Martha was inspired by the pattern name and chose fabrics with natural colors and textures for the Honeycomb Waffle and 3 Cubes blocks. Sky, green plants, rocks, and dirt appear in 3-D. We see ruins in a jungle. Martha made some blocks lighter and some blocks darker to achieve the look of strong sunlight or hidden shade.

ASTEROIDS *by Kathy Syring*

HOLLOW CUBE CLASSIC *by Kathy Syring*

Made from the second half of the strip piecing for the Arches and Asteroid blocks, this is a fun quilt. See page 50 for coordinating Arches quilt. Sara named the block for its floating effect. Kathy's color selection makes the quilt bright and cheery. A nice snuggle quilt for a crisp spring morning.

Kathy chose a collection of colors with an acid edge for her Hollow Cube quilt. Rather than making each block one color, in light, medium, and dark values, she chose sets of three different colors and made a few blocks from each set. One set is fuchsia with chartreuse and navy, one is gold with blue and dark purple, etc. All that matters is light, medium and dark for the 3-D effect, plus a color combination that pleases the beholder. Kathy had some fun with empty spaces, too. This is a sophisticated quilt.

NETCUBE *by Kristi Droese*

HILLTOPS *by Kathy Syring*

A black background makes these colors pop! The movement of the prints adds intrigue and playfulness to the design. What's around the corner, inside the next box? Kristi had fun playing with the addition of the single cubes at the top and bottom, too.

Kathy decided to go all the way with batik fabrics in this 3 Cubes quilt. Since the background fabric is dark, all the other fabrics must be a lighter shade, pushing the values in the cubes closer to each other. This very slightly reduces the 3-D effect, but it adds a radiant glow to the stacks of cubes. Also notice that she used more than one shade of black fabric. The visible seams and contrasting values bring out a crystalline effect, showing the construction of the quilt.

UPSY DAISY *by Martha Ethridge*

FLOATING ISLAND *by Pam Seaberg*

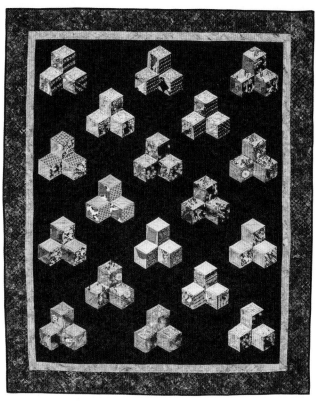

Shades of gray in black and white prints mix with bold colors, all light, medium, or dark. This is a great approach to choosing value. Start with no color as you are creating the blocks and then begin to drop in color. This pattern allows you to sew the half blocks together into a complete block, and then add a setting triangle of medium gray to the top and bottom. The blocks are sewn into columns, squared off at the top and bottom of each row. A great example of a medium value background. Polka dots and other stronger patterns add texture.

The 3 Cubes blocks alternate with Blank Space half hexagons to construct a nicely-spaced quilt layout. Pam obtains the 3-D illusion plus a glittery look from color choices and interesting larger prints. The sides of the cubes look like reflections of something else. The quilt has an atmospheric feeling.

SILK ROAD *by Marci Baker*

FUTURESCAPE *by Janet Blazekovich*

Here Marci is experimenting with larger prints and plaids. Somehow this is a piece with an Asian flavor. Enjoy a rich, mellow color scheme that flows like syrup. She combines Big Box with Sugar Cube to make a trail like rocks, mountains, and sand. The name is well chosen, since the designs and patterns are very silk-like. Sometimes a trip to a thrift shop will produce cottons with designs you have never seen before, perhaps intended for clothing or even furniture. Of course, different quilt shops can surprise you too. That's why we keep looking.

You could try a little sampler of 3-D blocks if you have project leftovers, or just for fun, since a few blocks take less time. This quilt mixes Big Box, Hollow Cube, Hole-in-One, Sugar Cube, and Blank Space half hexagons. Janet chose a dark background fabric with a multicolored pattern that looks like a night sky with stars. How many names could you think of for this composition? Meteor Shower, Planetary Resources, Modern Mall – hang this in an office, a kid's room, anywhere.

SINGULAR SAMPLER 1 *by Kristi Droese*

SINGULAR SAMPLER 2 *by Kristi Droese*

Kristi used white, gray, and black fabrics to create strong 3-D illusions. In fact, she did it twice, then added a bit of color to each. Color has an emotional content, and even a little affects the whole piece. Add the blue, and think of underwater ruins. But yellow and orange perhaps make you feel that you are seeing homes with supper cooking. Can you spot the block that Kristi put in upside down? Amazing how the mind sees the 3-D!

A TO Z *by Martha Ethridge*

CASINO *by Sara Nephew*

This colorful assortment of blocks is exciting in its enthusiasm. She's letting go. Primary colors, red, yellow, and blue, glow and sputter. It's hard to find light, medium, and dark when working with a radiant color like yellow. Those cubes glow like burning lanterns floating up into the sky. An occasional Honeycomb Waffle block, even a half-block, looks like a building corner among flowers or living, moving creatures. The more we look, the more we like it.

Sara made a larger group of blocks that mix and clash for a lot of action. It looks like fun and games like slot machines, dice, turning wheels, spinning chips. Among the dots and flower bursts are clever batiks from Scott Hansen. An artist who loves scraps, Sara started with a few Honeycomb Waffle blocks left over from another project, then made more in hotter colors. Hollow Cube blocks were the result of trying Marci's new measurements – many Hollow Cube blocks. Texture and detail were added with 3 Cubes and Sugar Cube blocks. Quilters, remember that the house always wins!

JAMBOREE *by Kate McIntyre*

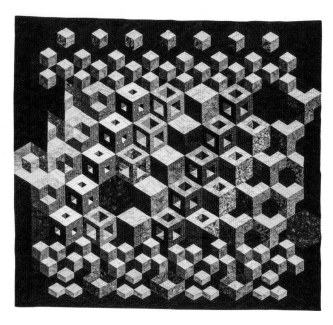

DIATOMS *by Kathleen Springer*

Once you get started, maybe you don't want to stop! Kate continued until she made some of every single block in this collection, using gorgeous color. She even made variations of the Hollow Cube. Pink Honeycomb Waffle blocks look good upside down too. Can you see the black holes in this universe? Finally, she created a balanced layout, with diagonal rows of color through the center, enclosed with straight lines of blocks across the top and bottom.

This underwater fantasy constructs giant kelp, coral, slanting rays of sunlight. Sea creatures, even microscopic diatoms, are so beautiful. Kathleen has captured that beauty, and the play of flickering light and shadow underwater. She has not always emphasized strong 3-D effects, but it is there in the twists and turns. Kathleen's cousin was a well-known and respected marine geochemist who studied undersea hydrothermal vent systems. Kathleen's inspiration was from many pictures her cousin had of the ocean floor. Very satisfying!

ARROWHEAD *by Kristi Droese*

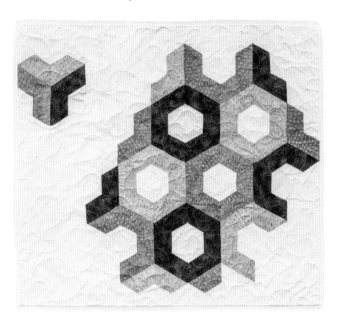

COLISEUM *by Kristi Droese*

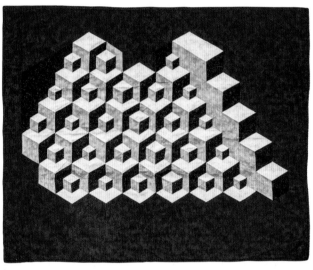

This is a small wall hanging that plays with the Arches block to make some interesting shapes. Kristi is designing, maybe losing the 3-D effect. But what if she kept on, making it bigger? It's fun to explore with her ideas – where would you go? Can you see how it goes together? Are you adventurous?

Kristi uses some of Marci's variations on the Honeycomb Waffle block – Bit 'O Honey and Honey Store – to construct ancient architecture. Black, white, and gray are stunning against intense red. Big Box blocks make a defensive wall

SARA'S STRETCH *By Sara Nephew*

HONEY QUILT *by Janet Blazekovich*

This quilt is mostly red, blue, and shades of gray with Hollow Cubes, 3 Cubes, and Honeycomb Waffle blocks. Sara added left and right horizontal strips to each half block to extend (stretch) the edge of the block, or contrast with it. This creates interesting shapes with and between familiar blocks. The striking border of batik encloses all the resulting shapes with white, blue, purple, and black in a dribbling vertical stripe.

Even though this quilt is made in shades the color of honey, using blocks named after honey, we're pushed into thinking of money, not honey. Bricks and blocks of gold! Very, very rich! You could recline on gold and lie under gold. In any case, this is an excellent quilt. Crisply 3-D with Bit o' Honey, Honeycomb Waffle, and Honey Store blocks, it has plenty of variety, though the color scheme is simple.

3-D SCRAPS *by Sara Nephew*

QUICK CHANGE *by Laurie Biundo*

After finishing the stretch quilt, it seemed a shame to leave out the leftover blocks. Luckily all the blocks easily fit together, so it was fun to lay them out and play with blocks until a pleasing arrangement resulted in a baby quilt (or wall hanging).

White, red, and black are often successful choices for a strong 3-D design. This is actually a more challenging puzzle, because a background fabric is also needed. Laurie chose a medium tone of a brown with contrast in the pattern. Both the pattern and the heat of the red color help the cubes pop out at the viewer – successful 3-D.

Cutting Shapes with Triangle Rulers

Here are some basic shapes which can be cut using the Clearview Triangle rulers. With each shape, make the first cut to establish a 60° angle. The shapes include seam allowances. Alternatively, you can cut shapes using the templates on pages 78–83.

TIP When Kate McIntyre was testing the 5″ blocks, she found that cutting the largest size strip first, stacking all three values, and then cutting the shapes was quite efficient. From there she reduced the strip width and cut the next size of shape. By doing this she was able to quickly cut the individual pieces for one block.

FIRST CUT

Cut a strip the size of the shape. At the right end of the strip, place the ruler with a point up and ¼″ line aligned with the lower edge of the strip. Cut along the right edge of the ruler.

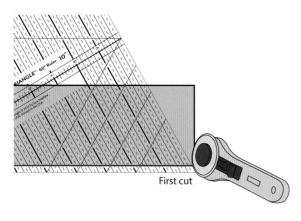

First cut

For easier and faster sewing, trim the 60° corners using Corner Cut 60 as marked with green lines on each shape.

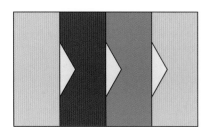

Light → Dark → Medium → Light

TRIANGLES

1. Make the first cut as shown in First Cut, at left.

2. Turn the angled end of the strip to the left.

3. With the ruler point down and left edge of the ruler at the left end of the strip, align the triangle size line along the top of the strip. The size line is the same as the strip width (3″ triangle is shown). Cut. Rotate the ruler and continue cutting triangles until you have the number needed for your project.

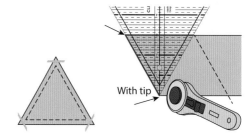

With tip

NOTE Triangles have a ½″ of fabric at the tip. It is helpful to know that only ¼″ of this fabric is needed for the seam allowance If you need a 3″ triangle out of a 2¾″ strip, you can get it. See the diagrams shown here for a triangle without the tip.

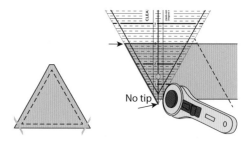

No tip

DIAMONDS

1. Make a cut as shown in First Cut, page 76.

2. Turn the angled end of the strip to the left.

3. Place the triangle at the left end with the top point to the lower left. Align the appropriate ruler line from the bottom of the ruler to cut the diamond at the same width as the strip (3" diamond is shown). Cut.

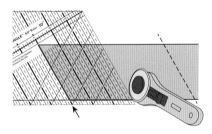

An alternate way to cut a diamond is to use the tip of the ruler. Align the ruler line along the base of the strip and at the left end. Cut on the right edge only.

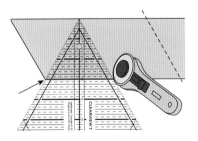

Continue cutting diamonds until you have the number needed for your project.

FLAT PYRAMIDS

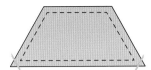

1. Make a cut as shown in First Cut, page 76.

2. Turn the angled end of the strip to the left. With the point of the ruler down, align the trapezoid size line along the top edge of the strip and the left edge of ruler along the left edge of the strip (4" flat pyramid cut from a 2" strip is shown). Cut.

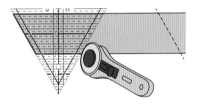

3. Rotate the ruler and continue cutting flat pyramids until you have the number needed for your project.

TRIANGLE HALVES

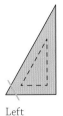

Left   Right

1. Cut the appropriate size rectangle given in the instructions (3⅜″ × 5¾″ fits a 9″ block).

2. Right: With the rectangle vertical and the centerline of the ruler along the left edge of the rectangle and the tip at the upper left corner, cut the rectangle from corner to corner diagonally.

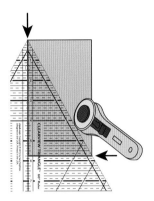

3. Left: With the rectangle vertical and the centerline of the ruler along the left edge of the rectangle and the tip at the lower left corner, cut the rectangle from corner to corner diagonally.

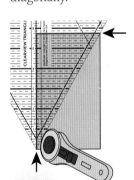

TIP To get left and right halves at the same time, place 2 rectangles, wrong sides together, and cut either right or left.

TIP If the ruler and fabric do not align correctly, do not twist the ruler to cut diagonally corner to corner, as this will not be the correct angle. Remeasure the rectangle and recut if needed.

TEMPLATES / ACTUAL SIZE SHAPES

Numbers in parentheses are quantities of that shape that can be cut from a 40″ strip of fabric.

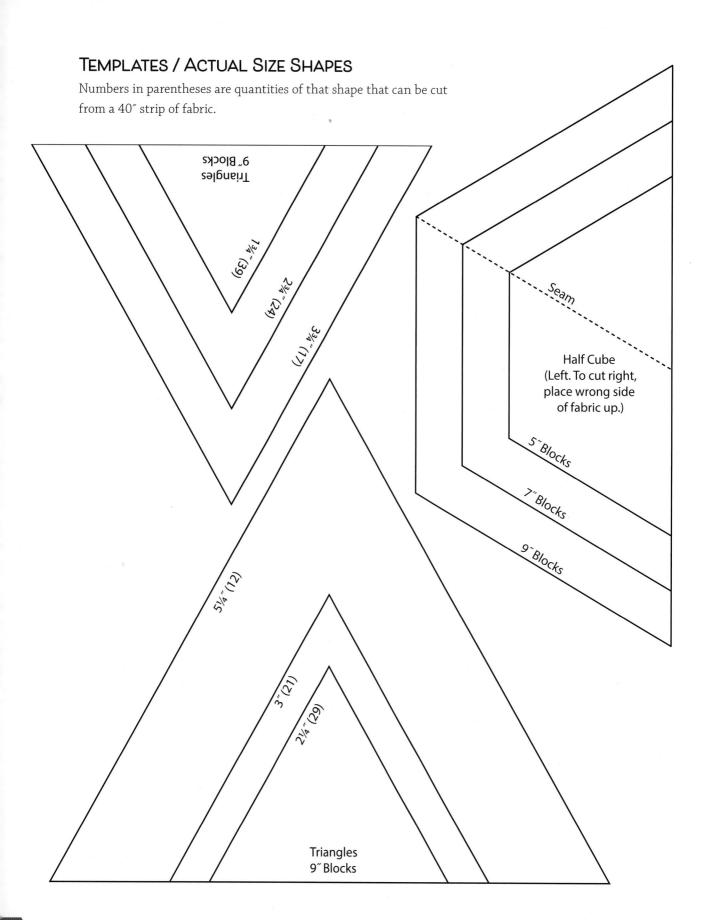

Triangles
9″ Blocks

1¾″ (39)

2¾″ (24)

3¾″ (17)

5¼″ (12)

3″ (21)

2¼″ (29)

Triangles
9″ Blocks

Seam

Half Cube
(Left. To cut right,
place wrong side
of fabric up.)

5″ Blocks

7″ Blocks

9″ Blocks

TEMPLATES / ACTUAL SIZE SHAPES

Numbers in parentheses are quantities of that shape that can be cut from a 40″ strip of fabric.

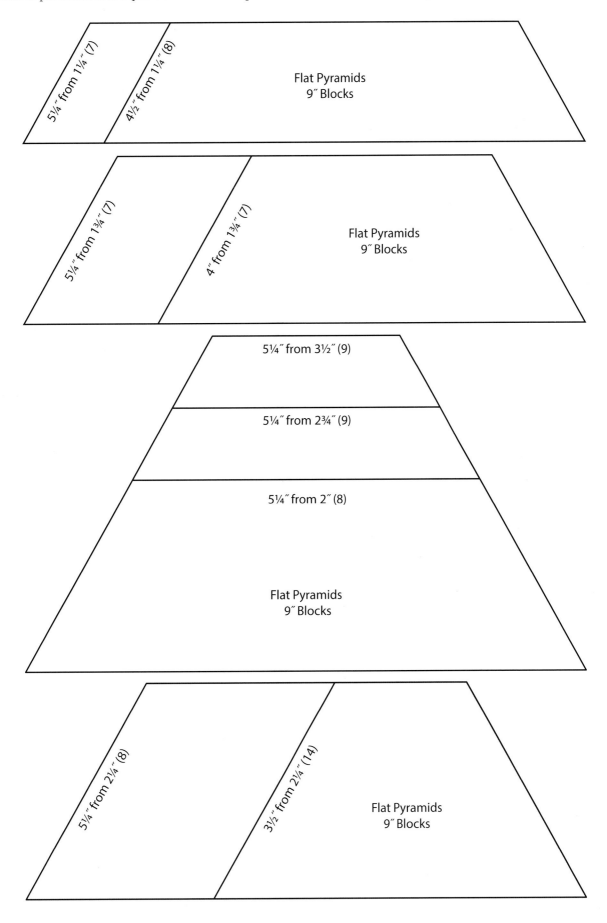

5¼″ from 1¼ (7)   4½″ from 1¼ (8)   Flat Pyramids 9″ Blocks

5¼″ from 1¾″ (7)   4″ from 1¾″ (7)   Flat Pyramids 9″ Blocks

5¼″ from 3½″ (9)

5¼″ from 2¾″ (9)

5¼″ from 2″ (8)

Flat Pyramids 9″ Blocks

5¼″ from 2¼″ (8)   3½″ from 2¼″ (14)   Flat Pyramids 9″ Blocks

TEMPLATES / ACTUAL SIZE SHAPES

Numbers in parentheses are quantities of that shape that can be cut from a 40″ strip of fabric.

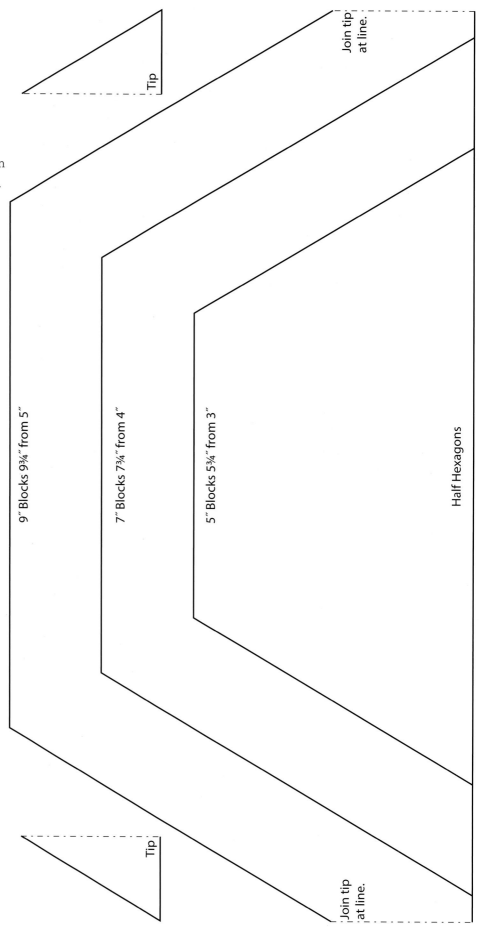

Tip

Join tip at line.

9″ Blocks 9¾″ from 5″

7″ Blocks 7¾″ from 4″

5″ Blocks 5¾″ from 3″

Half Hexagons

Tip

Join tip at line.

TEMPLATES / ACTUAL SIZE SHAPES

Numbers in parentheses are quantities of that shape that can be cut from a 40″ strip of fabric.

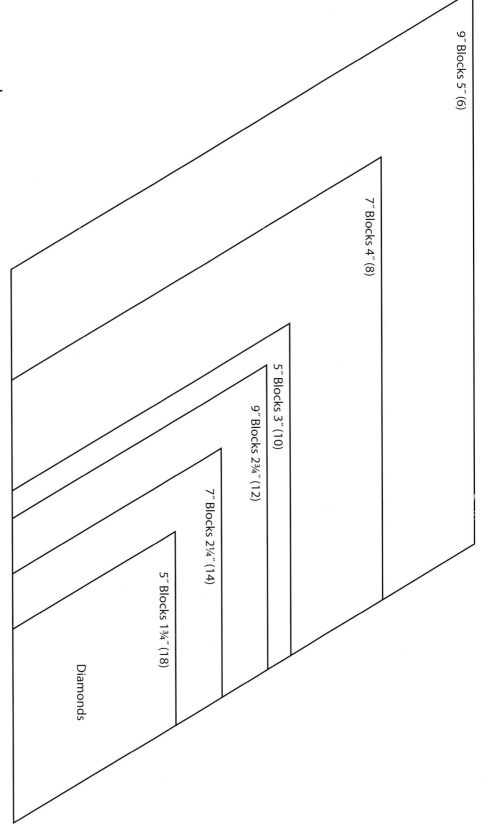

9″ Blocks 5″ (6)

7″ Blocks 4″ (8)

5″ Blocks 3″ (10)

9″ Blocks 2¾″ (12)

7″ Blocks 2¼″ (14)

5″ Blocks 1¾″ (18)

Diamonds

TEMPLATES

TEMPLATES / ACTUAL SIZE SHAPES

Numbers in parentheses are quantities of that shape that can be cut from a 40″ strip of fabric.

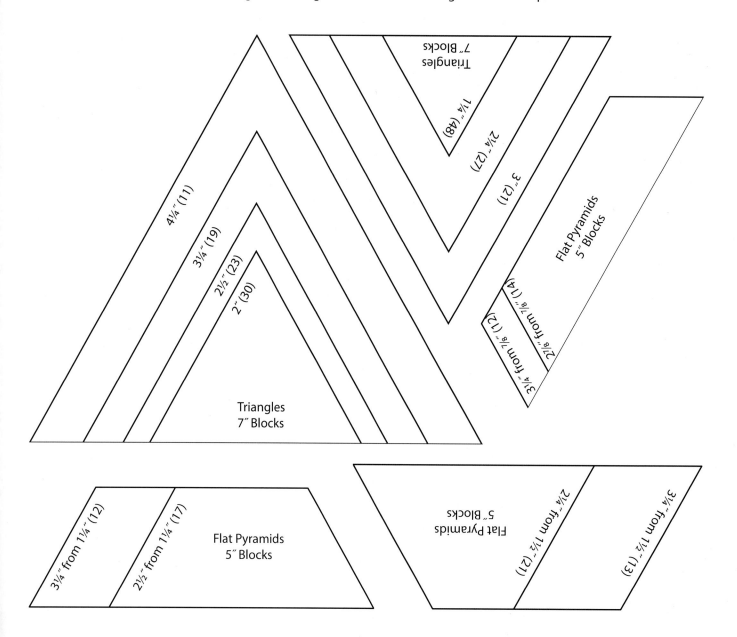

Triangle Halves (Right)

9″ Blocks 3⅜″ × 5¾″ (7 pairs)

7″ Blocks 2¾″ × 4¾″ (8 pairs)

5″ Blocks 2⅛″ × 3¾″ (10 pairs)

Triangle halves: Right is shown. Left is wrong side of fabric up.

Triangles 7″ Blocks

4¼″ (11)

3¼″ (19)

2½″ (23)

2″ (30)

1¼″ (48)

2¼″ (27)

3″ (21)

Triangles 7″ Blocks

Flat Pyramids 5″ Blocks

3¼″ from 7/8″ (12)

2⅛″ from 7/8″ (14)

3¼″ from 1¼″ (12)

2½″ from 1¼″ (17)

Flat Pyramids 5″ Blocks

Flat Pyramids 5″ Blocks

2¼″ from 1½″ (12)

3¼″ from 1½″ (13)

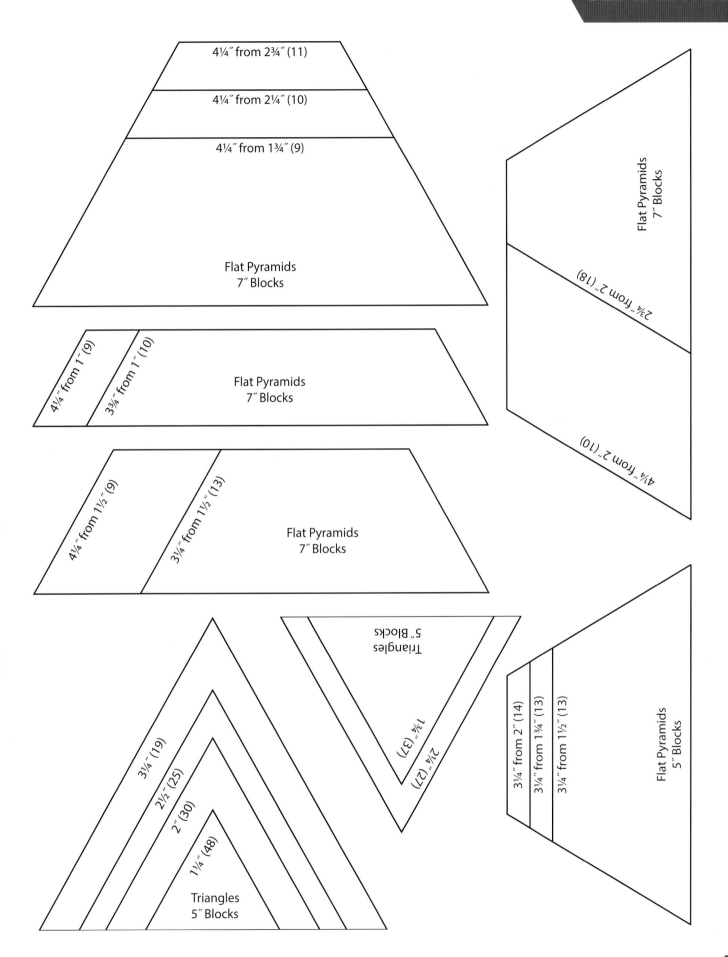

4¼″ from 2¾″ (11)

4¼″ from 2¼″ (10)

4¼″ from 1¾″ (9)

Flat Pyramids
7″ Blocks

Flat Pyramids
7″ Blocks

2¾″ from 2″ (18)

4¼″ from 2″ (10)

4¼″ from 1″ (9)

3¾″ from 1″ (10)

Flat Pyramids
7″ Blocks

4¼″ from 1½″ (9)

3¾″ from 1½″ (13)

Flat Pyramids
7″ Blocks

3¼″ (19)

2½″ (25)

2″ (30)

1¼″ (48)

Triangles
5″ Blocks

Triangles
5″ Blocks

1¾″ (37)

2¼″ (27)

3¼″ from 2″ (14)

3¾″ from 1¾″ (13)

3¼″ from 1½″ (13)

Flat Pyramids
5″ Blocks

To create your own design and play with the possibilities, we have included a grid and pages of the thirteen different blocks. Copy as needed and cut and paste the different designs. Make your own 3-D magic!

Copy the page, cut out the blocks, and create your own design.

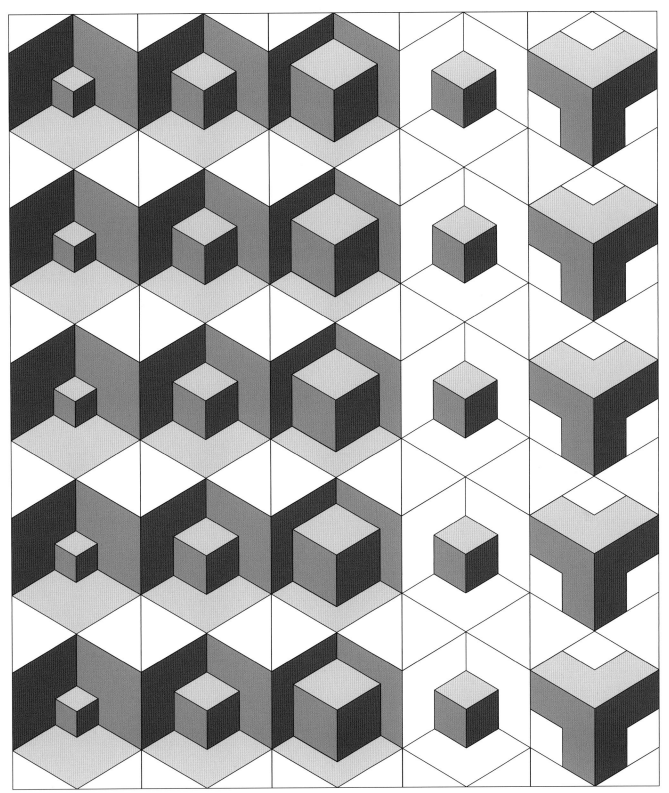

Bit O' Honey, Honeycomb Waffle, Honey Store, Asteroid, Arches

Copy the page, cut out the blocks, and create your own design.

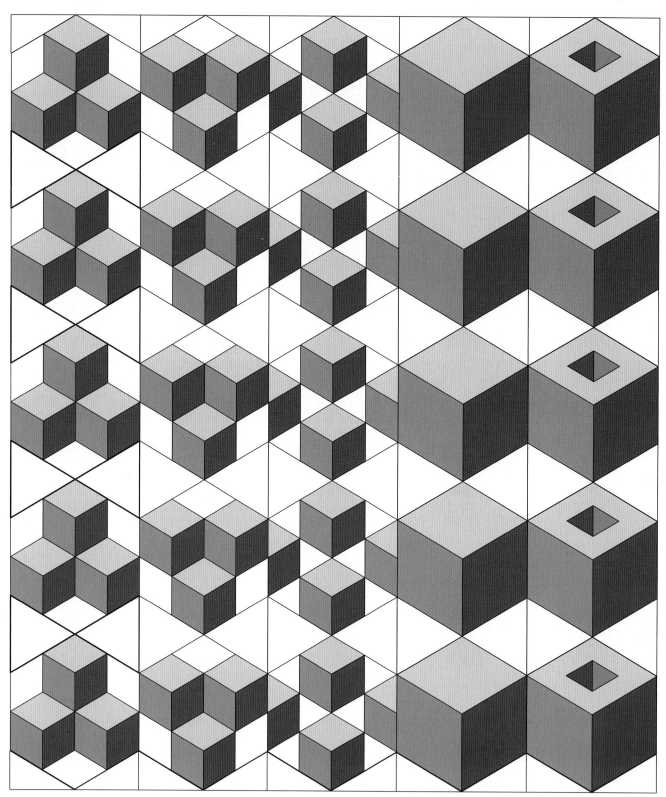

3 Cubes, Toss Up, Sugar Cube, Big Box, Hole-in-One (Top)

Copy the page, cut out the blocks, and create your own design.

Hole-in-One (Left), Hole-in-One (Right), Peek-A-Boo, Hollow Cube Classic, I-See-You

Copy the page, cut out the blocks, and create your own design.

MARCI BAKER

Recognized internationally for her expertise in quilting, Marci enjoys sharing ideas that simplify the quilting process. A native of Dallas, Texas, Marci began teaching quilting in 1989 for her local quilting guild and shops. In 1993, she started Alicia's Attic, a company that combines her love of math and teaching with her love of quilting.

As an admirer of traditional quilts, Marci was inspired to author the Not Your Grandmother's Quilts series, which uses traditional patterns that people associate with grandmothers but simplifies the techniques. In 2006, she expanded Alicia's Attic by purchasing Clearview Triangle from Sara Nephew. Marci and Sara are collaborating on new designs and techniques, with Marci traveling and teaching under her new business name: Quilt with Marci Baker. One of her latest adventures is developing instruction and presenting on C&T's Creative Spark, their online learning platform.

Marci and her husband, Clint, live in Fort Collins, Colorado, where they enjoy the beautiful mountain views. Contact Marci at marci@quiltmb.com.

Follow Marci on social media:

Website:
quiltwithmarcibaker.com
(Be sure to check out her latest schedule and sign up for her newsletter!)

Facebook: QuiltMB

YouTube: @MarciBaker

Instragram:
QuiltwithMarciBaker

SARA NEPHEW

Sara is a quilt designer, author, and teacher who has developed several isometric (60°) triangle rulers. Her quilting career has taken her all over the United States, Canada, and Australia, and her quilts have been widely exhibited. Sara has been featured in magazine articles and books.

Always an artist, Sara started her career as a commercial jeweler. She began learning diamond setting as well as continuing her work with painting and cloisonné enameling. After several other careers, Sara gravitated toward quilting and found her calling.

When Sara started the Clearview Triangle business, her multifaceted quilting career took off. In 2006, she retired from the day-to-day operations of running her business and sold her company to Marci Baker of Alicia's Attic. But Sara has not stopped working, creating new quilts, or writing—as evidenced by this book! Currently she is also having fun baking no-knead bread. Contact Sara at saranephew@quiltmb.com.

Also by Sara Nephew

Also by Marci Baker

Also by Marci Baker and Sara Nephew

Marci Baker photo by April Cantrell (Texas Sun Photography)
Sara Nephew photo by Rowland Studios